The Witness of Sin, a Theodicy

THE WITNESS OF SIN

THE WITNESS OF SIN

A THEODICY

BY
REV. NATHAN ROBINSON WOOD
MEDFORD, MASS.

New York   Chicago   Toronto
Fleming H. Revell Company
London and Edinburgh

CONTENTS

INTRODUCTION

IF there were not the strongest ties of natural affection as well as the bonds of Christian love between the author of this book and myself, I might speak more freely than propriety will now permit me.

Inability to reconcile the goodness of God with the existence of sin and all its dire consequences in this world where God is both immanent and transcendent has staggered many a soul and clouded its faith with doubt.

It seems to me that no difficulty in this most abstruse problem has been evaded in this discussion. Sophistries and casuistries have been stripped off and thrown aside. The real difficulties have been uncovered and met.

If the conclusions of this book are true, and I believe that they are, we may well thank God and take courage.

The riddle of Samson will have a new solution when applied to the existence of sin in the universe,

> "Out of the eater came forth food
> And out of the strong came forth sweetness."

NATHAN E. WOOD.

THE PRESIDENT'S HOUSE,
THE NEWTON THEOLOGICAL INSTITUTION,
August, 1905.

THE WITNESS OF SIN

I

GOD AND SIN

NO apology or preface is needed for the subject of sin in the world. Of all the problems which force themselves upon us as we look at human life, this is the greatest and most insistent. The evils of the world need no vivid and elaborate setting forth. They are the commonplace of rhetoric, and they speak for themselves with a thousand voices. But that which makes sin, with its myriad evils in society, in characters, in fortunes, the supreme problem of human life, is not the mere consequences of sin, awful as those are. That which makes sin not only the practical problem of life, but the supreme problem of the reason, is the fact that sin, this universal and vital reality, is in strange and terrible conflict with the supreme reality, which is God. In this defiance of God by sin lies the real problem. Sin is, and God is; but how can

both be in the same world? Each may seem
to deny the other, but the danger of the problem is that, to many, sin seems to deny God.
To many others it is a cloud upon the blaze
of His existence; and to all it is the profoundest problem contained in human life. The
existence of a supreme, a Divine, an all-good
and all-powerful Being, is the hope of the
world. But if God is the quest of the ages,
sin is the barrier of the ages. No problem or
perplexity, nothing except the actual working
of sin itself in their own souls, has kept so
many from seeing God as has this problem
of sin in His world.

Some sort of a theodicy, some showing of
the way in which sin may exist in the world
of an all-good and all-powerful God, becomes
a necessity, at least in any religious thinking.
The two highest of undivine religions have
made a theodicy their framework. Buddhism
fantastically represents the world as the evil
sloughed off from a good deity, and as des-
tined, with the dying of evil, to be reabsorbed
into deity, and to cease to exist. Zoroastrian-

ism made its theism a theodicy, depicting the
world as held in a gigantic balance of Good
and Evil, Ormuzd and Ahriman, each a deity,
with good victorious in the end. In the Bible
we find no framework of theodicy, for the purpose of the Bible is to do what no uninspired
religion has done, to deal with the practical
problem of sin, by showing man a way out
from sin. But except that it reveals infinite
truth about God and about sin, the Bible states
the problem of theodicy but once, in the Book
of Job, where it shows as its sublime solution
the overwhelming majesty of God and our
own ignorance of His ways. Butler's "Analogy," written in the light of the whole Bible
and of modern intellect, presents the same argument in the profoundest rational form.
"Paradise Lost" and Augustine's "City of
God" have made other aspects of the problem
a part of the world's thought. In the largest
sense these mighty works are theodicies.
But they have not sought to give a specific
answer to the direct question of theodicy,
"How can sin and an all-powerful God be

in the same world?" With the Bible, and after it the "Analogy," to show the folly of doubt because of sin; with the Bible, and after it "Paradise Lost," to show how sin entered the world; with the Bible, and after it the "City of God," to show God's dealing with sin in the world;—people still ask the question of theodicy, of the nature of God, the goodness and power of God, in view of sin.

A specific answer to that question has not been given, and to-day we face the problem more plainly than ever. For a time indeed the thinking world has left the theistic problems of the days of Leibnitz, Voltaire, Edwards, and Butler, and has been drawn away by the advance of physical science to what is not a problem, but a battle of opinions, the question of natural and supernatural. But while that conflict, like every conflict of opinions, has left both sides about where they were before, it has brought both sides back to the problem which has never ceased to be foremost in the popular mind, the problem of sin and God in the world. For there has arisen,

as a result of the generalisations of science, a
tendency to look at things in a cosmic way, to
think of the race rather than of individuals, of
the world rather than the race, and of the
universe rather than of this particular world.
And this cosmic thought, this largest view
of God's working in the world, brings us face
to face with the great unsolved problem of the
days of theistic and atheistic strife.   In this
large plan of God in the world sin presents
itself, a universal apparition, a defiant and undeniable reality.   To every theist this becomes
a supreme question.   We have had in these
days of science a vision of the Divine order
almost Pauline in its sweep.   What is the
place of sin in this order?   We behold, we
think, as never before, the hand of God in
nature.   Where is the hand of God in sin?
It may be said of this problem of theodicy, if
it may ever be said of any problem, that it
demands solution, for it belongs to actual life.
We do not have to evolve it for ourselves, like
certain problems of criticism, over which many
dervishes whirl themselves frantic.   It forces

itself upon us. Neither is it bewildered by the "anise and cummin" of dates and styles and words. It is as broad as the universe and as deep as human life. It is indeed the most human, the least abstract, of all the problems of philosophy. For this reason there is no problem which perplexes so many of the people who do not claim to be thinkers, but who nevertheless think, as this question of the existence of sin in the world. Even the thoughtless pause to ask it. It is a universal abstraction of the most concrete form. It is a paradox which actually exists. While abstruse, divine philosophy retires to its grove and strictly meditates the "highest good" or the "first principle," common philosophy, in the street and in the home, is ever propounding this problem, which stares one in the face: "How can sin and God both be true? How can they be in the same world?" There is no other enigma in philosophy, divine or undivine, of which the world so strictly demands a solution, for the problem demands it of the world. There are problems in religion

which are made what they are by the element
of infinity, which are forever seen by the soul,
but not grasped by the intelligence. The mystery of the Three in One is of this nature,
and the mystery of fixed fate and free will.
These parallels meet only in eternity. But
perspective plays no part in the mystery of sin
in the world. It is not a discrepancy, or a
gulf, between God and sin; it is a conflict, and
a shock of meeting. And this meeting-point
is not far off, beyond the ultimate outpost of
our thought. It lies within our own experience. Sin meets God in our own souls.

It is undoubtedly true that the problem of
evil is more likely to present itself to the stu-
dent of the natural world or to the average
man as a problem of natural evil, of pain, suffering, misfortune, sickness, and death. We
are all more puzzled over the evil which we
suffer than over the evil which we do. But all
the problems of evil rest upon the problem of
sin, and are explained by sin.

For the injustice and oppression which are
in the world, the inequalities of fortune, the

wicked prospering, the righteous failing, inno-
cence trampled upon and virtue cast down by
vice,—" and captive Good attending captain
Ill,"—all these things, which are to many persons the problem of life, are simply aspects of
the question of defiant sin: sin prospered and
triumphant for a time, for it is only for a time,
in defiance of God,—the sinful and the wicked
striking down the virtuous and oppressing the
innocent, in defiance of Divine justice.

And what we call natural evil, such as pain,
misery, sickness, the scientist sees as the direct
or indirect result of moral evil in ourselves, or
in our ancestors, or in society at large. The
Scriptures add to this summing up of the
natural evils which are the harvest of sin, that
sin is the seed of death. But if natural evil
may undoubtedly be traced to sin as its source,
this but adds to the burden of the problem of
sin.

Beyond this, natural evil reveals itself
clearly to modern eyes as a punitive force. In
pain, misery, and privation, even in an earth
discordant in her fairest scenes, sown with

suffering, and red with blood, moral order appears at its corrective work. Purifying power blows in it like a destroying wind through miasms. He is blind who to-day cannot see in natural evil the divine order of the universe asserting itself against sin. But sin, with this divine machinery of trouble arrayed against it, is more a problem than ever. What shall we say of that which calls for the correction, which needs the punishment, which leaves the debris to be purified? What shall we say of that sin against which the divine order of the universe must assert itself? Sin stands a blacker mystery than ever in the light which shines through natural evil. It is not hard for the theist to see, back of natural evil, God, arraying the universe against moral evil. A recent writer [1] has drawn the philosophy of natural evil into a phrase and set forth God's personal relations to natural evil, when he says: "Suffering is God's protest against sin." But what shall we say of sin? In this tremendous indictment of sin by the voice of all natural evil, appears more awful than ever the power

[1] Principal Fairbairn.

and antagonism of that sin against which God must protest!

This problem of sin, though it lies in man's nature, is far more profound than the problem of the origin of sin in man. It is indeed strange that man could have sinned. For we cannot believe that God created man with sin, or the seeds of sin, in him. How then did sin begin in a sinless being? But we can point to the free will of man, which explains how man could have sinned, if not why he should have sinned. Sin was not impossible to man. This problem is shallow beside the deeper problem of sin and God. A sinless being, with freedom of will, has power to sin, and the occurrence of sin in the soul of a being who, though sinless, had power to choose between love of God and love of sin, is immeasurably less mysterious than the occurrence of sin in the world of a God who must forever hate sin.

This problem of sin is also in every way more vital than the question of the origin of sin in man. For tracing the origin of sin cannot change the fact of sin. Sin, however it got here, is here, and the real and vital question before men is, not how sin got here, but how to get rid of it. But in order to get rid of it, God is necessary; and the problem is that sin, by its presence in His world, obscures God, and to some seems even to deny Him. It is a question not of our past, but of our future, because it is a question of God. Sin has already affected the nature of man; shall we let it affect the nature of God for us? Shall we let it raise an unanswered question of the goodness and power of God? God, by the very idea of God, must be perfect in goodness, but sin in His world is evil. He must be perfect in power, but sin defies Him. This problem of theodicy, of defiant sin and God, arising out of the actual world, from the conflict of these two great realities in our own souls, intensified by the revealing light of natural evil, and swallowing up the question of the origin of evil, is the most insistent, the most vital, the most profound, and indeed the only, problem which stands between our intelligence and God.

II

EVASIONS

WHEN this question, "How can sin and God both be in the same world?" presents itself, there are many who would meet it by evasion. And the only way to do this is to deny that God and sin do both exist. Which of the two one denies depends mostly upon things outside of one's self. A mind prone to see but one thing at a time, or inclined to meet problems by evasion, may equally well become pessimist or pantheist. If such a mind is brought up in an atmosphere of naturalism or of materialism, it easily meets the appearance of sin by denying the existence of God. If such a mind has been cradled in the church or fed upon a mild philosophy, it gets faith by denying the reality of sin. Such pessimism, which is atheism, and such optimism, which is pantheism, are kith and kin. They are both of them evasions of the great problem of the world.

Atheism is no longer what it once was as a compact force and a definite theory. The glitter of Voltaire, the sword-play of Bayle, the lucid fallacies of Hume, are not of our day. It is a far cry, even from such thinking as theirs, to that recent well-paid apostle of atheism, the climax of whose philosophy was the question, superfluous to all who knew the work of the questioner, "If the devil should die, would God make another?" Atheism, at the present day, if it is to be found in the form of thought, must be looked for rather in the guise of extreme agnosticism or of the theatrical pessimism of Schopenhauer. Pessimism is in fact the real atheism of to-day, and pessimism is an atheism which, unlike the older atheism, is founded entirely upon the evil which is in the world. In Schopenhauer this theme of evil in the world plays second part to a strange and gigantic self-conceit. But in his followers, such as von Hartmann, the denial of God because of evil is the burden of their pessimism.

The world is very bad, and there is, therefore,
no God; there is only a blind and remorseless
Will. As a recent writer has well said, they
talk as though they had made the world, long
ago in their youth, but had well repented of
it. Such a denial of God is to any rational
mind simply a weak evasion of the supreme
problem of God and sin. It is no more irrational than the denial of the reality of sin,
but it is more foolish from the practical point
of view, for it loses all that could be gained by
an evasion. One may seek, even by evasion,
to see beyond dispute the existence of God;
but no one cares for the undisputed existence
of sin.

If we are seeking a theodicy, or an optimism based upon the facts in the case, atheism
and pessimism do not lie in our road. We
shall have dealt with them sufficiently if we
find the answer to them in a solution of the
problem. But the kind of false optimism which
rests on a denial of the reality of sin does en-
cumber the way to a true and reasoned optimism or to a true theodicy. The optimism of

a true theodicy cannot be confused by pessimism, but it may be by false optimism. One is not obliged to clear away this false optimism, yet for the sake of the best understanding of the problem it is well to analyse these evasions of the problem by the denial of sin.

Those whose faith is not strong enough to lay hold upon God in spite of sin, and whose moral sense is so weak that sin in themselves does not lead them to the realisation of God, may find the denial of sin almost a necessity of the religious life. Of these there is little to be said. It is a personal matter with them, a necessity of their weakness. But wherever the denial of sin is set forth as a philosophy of the universe, it takes its place in a strange harmony by the side of pessimism, the atheism which is founded on evil, as a twin evasion of the problem of sin and God. We need not of course force this kinship too far, and try to make it identity. For the complete parallel to the belief that there is no perfect Being above is the belief that there is no imperfection here below, and very few would deny that there is at least some imperfection in human society. The denial of sin comes rather in the affirmation that there is no sin in the positive sense, as a moral evil defiantly and successfully opposing itself to God. Sin is explained as a negative thing, as a natural evil, as an imperfection. It stands no longer as the antithesis of God.

Probably the extreme form of this view is found in that theory of the world which we call pantheism. Pantheism knows no evil in the world, as atheism knows no God. Pantheism has, however, its own ends before it, and its view of sin springs less from a conscious desire to evade the problem of evil than from a philosophy oblivious to aught but itself. Certain forms of pantheism, which might almost equally well be called atheism, see no defiant evil in sin because they see no personal moral Being to defy. Those, however, like Spinoza, whose pantheism is theistic, who, to put it roughly, would not put everything in place of God, but would see God as the essence of all things, are equally forced to exclude sin as a

reality from their divinely-intoxicated universe. Sin may somehow be in a world which
belongs to God, but it cannot be in a world
which is a part of God. God and sin may both
be true, but pantheism and sin certainly cannot. Therefore the pantheist denies sin, and
therefore also the world denies pantheism.

Next after pantheism the place in philosophy
from which the denial of the reality of sin has
been most often drawn is the *Theodicée* of
Leibnitz, perhaps the most celebrated of all
treatises upon the problem of sin. Leibnitz
is one of the great names in philosophy, one
in the line of hundred-handed geniuses, with
Aristotle, Leonardo, Bacon, and Goethe. In
his *Theodicée*, the fruit of a mind and temper
unique for boldness, confidence and brilliance,
ideas, arguments, metaphors, and illustrations
crowd one another. The result is that side by
side with a truly sublime conception and a
really profound argument he has left many
vague phrases about sin as " imperfection " or
" limitation," which obscure the large structure of his thought. The great idea of the

Theodicée was that this world is the "best possible world." Now evil is in this world, and the presence and permission of evil here must be explained before it becomes clear that this is the best possible world. Leibnitz showed by analysis how evil could have come into the world. Man is finite. Metaphysically he falls short of infinite completeness or perfection. This limitation inborn in finite power, intellect, knowledge, Leibnitz calls metaphysical imperfection. Physical evil he explained as conditionally a good, not good in itself, but good seen in its context in the book of human life, where it appears as a corrective of sin. But this moral evil, or sin, which is not mere finiteness, and beside which natural evil is a good, was the real problem before him. And Leibnitz argued that moral evil is the result of this finite imperfection as it affects the moral nature. From this argument there grew many eloquent phrases about moral evil as "imperfection," or "limitation," or a "mere failure of perfectness." In this of course he confounded quality and quantity.

The moral nature need not be infinite in quantity in order to be perfect in quality, that is, to be good. Nevertheless these phrases, the rhetoric of Leibnitz, have flown far more widely than his sober thought has gone. The thought of Leibnitz is that this finite imperfection, which works in all man's nature, works especially in the will of man. In the will of man, evil, before but a limitation of being, becomes moral, defies God, and is sin. The human will, he declares, is the source of sin, and finite limitation is but the occasion of it. Otherwise God, who is the author of this limitation, is responsible for sin. But Leibnitz declares that God in no way created sin; for while sin is made possible by this finite limitation, nothing but a will can give sin reality; it cannot be God's will which does this; it is man's will, which sins in defiance of God. This is the main point of his argument about the origin of evil as it concerns the Creator. To show how sin could begin in a being created sinless, he finds some such influence as finite imperfection a necessity. But

this would but charge the Creator of the finite
soul with being the creator of sin, did Leibnitz not throw his strongest emphasis upon the
fact that sin, made possible by finiteness, is
itself wholly the work of the human will, a
direct and positive evil, a defiance, not an incomplete attainment, of righteousness.

All this is, however, but a part of his more
famous theory in regard to the present permission of sin in the world. Looking not at
man's nature alone, but at the world at large,
he declares that evil is necessary to the "pre-
established harmony" of the universe. In itself not good, it is necessary as a foil to that
which is good, and which without its foil
would not be perfect. Sin is the shadow, the
darkness, without whose contrast the light
would lose half its brightness. This rhetoric,
though not new in itself, nor in its idea of
sin as a necessary part of a divine harmony,
took original and logical form in his celebrated
argument that this world is the "best possible
world," because the "best possible world" is
one containing sin. This greatest conception

of Leibnitz is not, as many who employ it now seem to think, simply an enthusiastic and defiant yelp of optimism in the face of sin. By it Leibnitz means, and this is the greatest development of his *Theodicée,* that the "best possible world" is a moral world, one containing "morality," or moral agents, and in such a world there is always a possibility of sin. He does not say of the best possible world, as he said of his pre-established harmony, that sin is necessary to it. He says only that sin is a necessary possibility in it. For where there are free wills, God cannot absolutely prevent sin. Sin may come to pass in such a best world, as it has in this one, in spite of God, and God is not to be blamed for it. The whole argument rests then upon moral defiance of God as the real nature of sin, and here is his whole explanation of sin. The origin of sin is not with God, but in the free will of man in defiance of God. Sin's continued presence in the world is not to be made a charge against God, since it is here because the free will sins in spite of God. And the

creation of such a world with such free wills
in it is not a cloud upon God's goodness, since
such a world, with free agents in it, is the best
possible world. The argument of the *Theodicée* turns at every point then upon the fact
that sin is positive moral evil, born of the free
will in defiance of God. But the mind of
Leibnitz was a restless and ardent one. He
desired to storm the problem with every wea-
pon at once. His great argument moves in a
cloud of phrases about "limitation," "imperfection," "negations," "shadows." And his
very phrase, "sin as a part of the best world,"
which to him means wholly that sin defies God
in the best world, is taken by the thoughtless,
and by the wilful, to mean that sin as a part
of the best world is itself not really evil.

But the idea of sin as a negation, an im-
perfect existence of good, or a mere absence
of good, does not depend upon Leibnitz, nor
for that matter upon any philosophy, or even
upon logic. It has its own philosophy, which
consists of illustrations, some of which have
done long and hard service down to the present

day. Sin, it is said, is not positive moral evil,
but a mere negation; not a force, but an absence. It is like cold, the absence of heat. It
is like shadow, the absence of light. It is a
vacuum, where good is not. These, which are
merely illustrations of an evasion of a great
reality, do not in themselves deserve much attention. But they are so common, and so
often take the place of reason and logic, that
it may be well to consider what force they
really have. Now illustrations have not the
force of proofs unless they are analogies as
well as illustrations. These illustrations of
shadow and cold and vacuum set forth a condition of negation, from which positive force,
light, or heat, is gone. They show then what
is meant when it is said that sin is a mere negation. But they do not show that sin is itself
such a negation as cold and shadow are, unless
they do so by analogy. And there is no force
of analogy in them in that direction. For
used as analogies, as anyone may use them,
they on the contrary sweep away all idea of
sin as negation. Is sin really not a positive

evil force, but only an absence of the good
divine force? What causes the absence then?
Is sin merely a vacuum of goodness? Material nature abhors a vacuum, and Divine
Nature and goodness must at least equally ab-
hor one; it must have come to pass in spite
of them; what defiant thing causes the
vacuum? Is evil like shadow, the absence of
light? What then casts the shadow from before the Divine righteous light? Is evil like
cold, the absence of heat? What is it which
stops at one point the heat of Divine love
which floods the universe? Something real
must cast the shadow and chill the heat. That
something, whatever it is, is sin. Two nega-
tives make a positive, say the grammarians.
It takes two positives to make a negative in a
real and positive world. It takes a positive
of tremendous power to cause a negation of a
positive God anywhere in His universe. If
sin is the negation of good, it must be a very
real and positive existence. It must be, as
Augustine says, a negation as fire is a negation. It creates the vacuum of goodness in

which it dwells. It casts its own shadow. It is foolish to say that sin is but the shadow, which something else casts, for if something else casts the shadow, that something else, which stops the light of God, or rather that stoppage itself, is the sin. The sin which does all this is in defiant opposition toward God. For a negation cannot be in a positive universe of positive Power and Love without positive opposition to that Power and Love— and, in fact, successful opposition, since, if unsuccessful, it could not exist. No deeper description can be given of the terrible antagonism of sin toward God than this, that sin, wherever it exists, casts a shadow from His light, and dispels the warmth of His love, and is the negation of His righteousness.

These phrases about sin as negation were very dear to that school of pantheists whose prophet was Emerson. Not a great figure in himself, Emerson is the best representative of the optimism which rests wholly upon the denial of sin. For those who deny sin often draw their optimism from the nature, the

love, and the universal presence of God.
Emerson on the other hand bases nothing
upon the nature and the presence of God, and
indeed says very little about God. His optimism is based upon the perfection and the glory
of human nature, and has for its corner stone
the creed that " evil is merely privative, not absolute," or that it is only so much " nonentity."
But this creed was itself a little too much a
negation or a nonentity for a foundation of
his optimism, and he strengthened it, or at
least filled it out, by the positive doctrine,
which he had partly from his masters before
him, partly from his own temperament, that
sin is good. Sin, it seems to him, is a positive good in its results, and even in itself.
Every sin, he said, is an incident on the upward path. Man grows sinless by the simple
method of committing sins, and so being done
with them. Man's crimes and misdeeds are
the processes through which he passes to
higher life. Sin is a growth toward goodness.
The evil spirits are on the road to heaven.
" Man, though in brothels, or jails, or on gib-

bets, is on his way to all that is good and true."
Most amiably, and with no real personal in-
tention, Emerson declares with Satan in
"Paradise Lost," "Evil, be thou my good."

Emerson had no desire to pose as a logical
thinker, nor, in the strictest sense, as a philosopher. Sifting out from the mass of his quo-
tations the ideas which were his own, one
finds that they are rather intuitions, percep-
tions, feelings, than ideas. In other words, he
meant to be, and is called, a seer, and as such
he was typical of a certain class of optimists,
mystics, minor poets, and vague pantheists,
who deny the reality of sin, and who are called
seers, doubtless because they are not reasoners
Very different from them in their vision of
sin, and from Emerson, who could not see sin
and said very little of any vision of God, are
the true seers of the race, who see sin because
it is real, and see God because He is real, and
see both with a vividness beyond the habit of
common men. Such were the sacred seers.
The more rapt their vision of God became, the
sterner grew their sense of sin, the more burn-

ing their words, the heavier the burden of
their prophecy. Such were the secular seers
of the race, the great poets,—Homer, with his
Iliad of woes, of battle, and of wrath,—Dante,
with his circles of fire and of frost, and his
steeps of Purgatory,—Shakespeare, master of
all the deeps of tragedy, passion, and guilt,—
and Milton, whose theme was the entrance of
sin and ruin into the world. They were seers,
not dreamers. 'And with them are the trage-
dians, Aeschylus, Sophocles, Euripides, and
their successors, whose theme is the punishment of sin. 'And even Goethe, the poet of
pantheism, rose to master-greatness only when
he traced, in Faust, the struggle of the human
soul, and the course of sin and its outcome,
and fell again from that high company when
in his second Faust he returned to his pantheism. It is time that we, the heirs of these
ages, ceased to give the name of seer to those
whose only title to it is that they cannot see.

As for Emerson and his paradox that sin
is good because its results are good, and because we grow upward by it, the best and the

only needed criticism is close at hand, in Emerson himself. If man grows better by evil, and every sin makes him, not more sinful, but less sinful, every descent raises, not lowers him, how did Emerson himself in his quiet, domestic, religious life come to the good character he had? And how does the man who passes through successive stages of deceit, lying, petty stealing, ruffianism, housebreaking, violent robbery, and murder, and from impure thought, through impure deed, to constant lust, debauchery, and riot of senses, come at the end to character so low morally and spiritually?

Emerson's thought, except that which he quoted, is not the kind which belongs to every age and generation. The virtue or vice, for us, in his theory of sin, is that it has outlasted all his good advice and his high-strung ecstasies, and that his phrases about sin, at once the basis and the weakest point of his philosophy, are the catchwords of to-day. For the theory of moral evolution, which in its extreme form has taken the place of Transcendentalism, is

Emerson's idea of upward growth through evil, expanded into a whole philosophy of the universe. Emerson's idea, and the theory called by the name of evolution, are indeed but the one and old idea, common to all ages, of a world perfected, or saved, or whatever one will, by mere process of growth. This natural fallacy of the human heart has seized the idea of evolution and bent it to its own ends. The race of men, it says, is steadily rising, one generation upon another, toward perfection. "Sin is the brute-inheritance" which we carry with us from our earthy origin. War, murder, lust, cruelty, crime, and misery are incidentals in the upward process through which the race attains at last the perfected condition which is "salvation." Or, in its partly Christian form, this view reads that through this vast evolutionary process God's infinite will is working out His universal plan. In the midst of this process we sin. But our sin, aimed against God though it may be, is but a part of His vast scheme, in which even sin is an accepted process. All things, good or bad,

are working together to this great consum-
mation of a race grown at last into perfect
and divine life. It is clear that all this gives
room for varying views of sin. The view
which comes nearest to Christian doctrine, for
instance, is that sin is an undeniable evil, an
unavoidable part in the process, which God
permits as a means of greater good. This is
the only real theodicy of evolution worthy of
study in its own place, and by no means
meant for a denial of the reality of sin. But
the evolutionist who, like the most popular
teachers of the philosophy, is at most a theist
or pantheist, and has imbibed no religious
hatred of the idea of sin, looks upon sin as a
mere incidental in the evolutionary process.
Sin is to him really a good, leading us upward,
or at the worst it is but imperfection, with the
hope of perfection in it. The sins which seem
obstacles are but stepping-stones, and every
fall, as John Fiske says, is a fall upward. It is
in tune with Emerson's theme, that the evil
spirits are on their way toward heaven, and
that mankind is advancing through gibbets

and jails to the good and the true. This is the end. Many in all ages have tried to think that sin is not evil. The theory that sin is a means of good is old. But there remains the last denial of sin, that sin is not evil, but a positive good. This is the death of reason, and the burial of ethics.

Little need be said of this last denial of sin. If sin is a positive good, why is the perfected race without it? Why must it not remain to keep the race in its perfected state, having once brought it there? If sin is not hateful to God, why is He leading the race through toil and travail so immense and infinite out of it? If sins are stepping-stones upward for the race, why are they steps downward for the individual? If every fall is a fall upward, why does the individual go downward in his fall? If continued sin helps to bring the race into light, why does it bring the individual to ruin of body and black despair of soul? The climax of the denial of God is the creed of the pessimist, that God, if there be a God, is evil. The climax of the denial of sin is that sin,

which defies God, is good. In these para-
doxes reason goes mad. "The fool," it was
declared, "hath said in his heart, 'There is no
God;'" no one had as yet thought to deny the
reality of sin. The moral result of both fol-
lies is the same. Atheism, it has been said, if
it could be made universal and practical, would
destroy society, for it would destroy morality.
Certainly the same is even more plainly true
of the denial of the reality of sin. If it could
be made universal and practical, it would destroy all law, all restraint, all ethics, all morality. Society would evolve itself through un-
hindered crime into chaos and death.

But worse than the moral result of either
folly of denial is the rational result. The
great problem of sin and God cannot be evaded
save at the ruin of all reason and certainty.
If we deny the reality of God, whose existence
is a universal intuition of the race, can we be
sure that it is not our own reason which has
lost its hold upon realities? And on the other
hand, if we declare that the universal consciousness of sin, so visible in and about us, is

at fault, how can we trust the universal consciousness, or our own consciousness, of God, whom we cannot touch or see? Reason feeds upon realities, and without them it dies. He who denies God or sin declares himself blind. He is no guide for the great problem. If there is a passage, as there must be, between the power of God and the power of sin, those Cyanean rocks which continually meet and shake the world, these blind guides are not the pilots for it. Atheism will be wrecked at last upon the indignant power of God, and blind optimism will be dashed, after a life of bland and lulled belief, upon the deadly rock of sin.

III

FACING THE PROBLEM

THE only thing to do with so great a
problem as that of sin and God is to
face it. Nothing of permanence, except perhaps one's own fate, will ever be
brought to pass by denying God or sin. If we
would seek either a solution of the problem or
a rational attitude toward it, we must face the
problem fairly and admit the reality of the
facts which constitute it. And this does not
mean the careless attitude which does not deny
these realities because it takes no thought at
all in regard to them. We must face them
seriously and sanely as realities. This is the
attitude of reason and the only way to a true
solution of the problem.

If it were not that we can face this problem
hopefully, even when we cannot penetrate it,
we should be badly off indeed. But it is possible to look upon it in a large and serious way,

grasping all the realities, and standing firm, by
faith. Like the Gordian Knot, this problem
must be either unravelled or cut, by one who
desires mastery over the world of his own
thinking. But faith cuts this knot, legitimately, and as by divine power. Faith is the
strongest and most rational attitude which one
can take in the presence of this problem. It
is the opposite of that weakness of mind which
must deny one or the other of the two great
realities, of that spirit of despair which cannot believe in God because of sin, and of that
other spirit of despair which cannot believe in
Him unless it denies sin. Faith is the true
realism, which believes in both visible realities.
It has in this matter the same spirit with the
truest science, for it acknowledges facts simply
because they are facts, and before they are explained. As Mephistopheles declared himself
the "spirit that denies," so on the other hand
faith is the spirit that affirms. It is this spirit
of faith, of realism, of science, of honesty,
which has cut the knot of our condition, even
though, as Pascal says, "it takes its twists and

turns in the abyss." It is this highest reason, this faith in God in spite of sin, which has redeemed the modern world from the despair of Greece and Rome. The wisest are those who live by faith, who can see the black expanse of sin and yet see that a God shines in the universe.

If this attitude of faith, of facing the problem and acknowledging its realities, is the highest reason, it is not surprising that the best logical treatments of the problem of sin should consciously or unconsciously have been reasoned statements of faith. For faith in this case means not only religion, but reason and sanity. The best of all these reasoned statements of faith is Butler's, in his great "Analogy," especially as found in the seventh chapter: "Of the Government of God Considered as a Scheme or Constitution Imperfectly Comprehended." Analogy and reason show, he says, that as the natural scheme of things is beyond us at many points, so also we are ignorant of the complete outlines of the moral plan of God in this universe; and that so, knowing His love and righteousness, we must believe, and have no ground but ignorance for not believing, that this moral order, in which sin has to be a possibility, and is a reality, is for the best in God's infinite plan. " The analogy of His natural government suggests and makes it credible that His moral government must be a scheme quite beyond our comprehension; and this affords a general answer to all objections against the justice and goodness of it."—"It is easy to see how our ignorance, as it is the common, is really a satisfactory answer to all objections against the justice and goodness of Providence."

This is evidently a logical statement of reason for trust in God in face of the mystery of sin. We do not know God's plan, but we do know His justice and goodness; and proceeding, in the only rational way, upon what we know, we must believe that God's plan is good and just, and that it is only our ignorance which keeps us from clearly seeing that it is so. On any ground this is unassailable logic. It

does not solve the mystery of sin, but it destroys any attacks, which the sight of sin may
inspire, upon the goodness and justice of God.
It shows that only ignorance can assail God,
and reveals faith as the very highest attitude
of reason.

And we find the rational attitude consciously
expressed again, in somewhat rigidly Calvinistic form, by perhaps the profoundest and
most comprehensive mind in America since
Jonathan Edwards. "Our great ground of
confidence, however, is the assurance that the
Judge of all the earth must do right. Sin is,
and God is; therefore the occurrence of sin
must be consistent with His nature; and as its
occurrence cannot have been unforeseen or un-
designed, God's purpose or decree that it
should occur must be consistent with His holiness."[1]   This setting forth of the rational attitude toward God is less satisfactory than
Butler's, because it attempts to make the argument explain the cause of sin, and nothing is
more characteristic of what Gladstone called
the "integrity" of Butler than his unfailing

[1] Hodge: Theology.

knowledge of how much an argument would prove.

But while we find the attitude of faith and of facing the problem consciously expressed by one or two, we find it more often unconsciously expressed, as for instance in a recent able work,[2] where it is put not as a statement of the reasonableness of faith, but as a theory of theodicy. The argument in that work is that since God is infinite Reason, and works according to laws of wisdom and love, we may be certain that if He does not prevent sin it is because He cannot in accordance with those laws. This is in reality a very clear presentation of the rationale of faith in God, and, as such, is better than many a mistaken theory of theodicy, but it is not itself a theory of theodicy, and does not, as it claims, "explode the dilemma" of sin, except by faith. For it is a statement of belief that God has good reason, in the law of His nature, for not preventing sin. If it stated what that reason is, and how it affects the law of God's nature, it would be a

[2] Harris: "God Creator and Lord of all."

theory of theodicy.   As it is, it is what is next
best to a true theory of theodicy, a setting forth
of the only rational attitude toward God.

This same reason, of faith in God, has been
the vital principle of the three most complete
attempts that have been made at an ordered
theodicy.   The first of these is the *Theodicée*
of Leibnitz.   The large Optimism of Leibnitz
beheld God, the all-good and all-wise, planning the world, and selecting, out of the endless number of worlds which existed in idea, one, which was the best possible world, and which He caused to exist in reality.   And
though sin exists in this world, yet we must
believe, and we cannot deny or disprove, that
this world, since God selected it, is the best
world possible.   This is the rational and consistent optimism of the *Theodicée,* and, in its
breadth and philosophic structure, irradiated
by genius, it still stands alone.   This optimism
is not itself a theory of theodicy, and when
Leibnitz came to construct a theodicy upon it,
and to explain how this is the best possible
world, as one containing morality and hence

the possibility of sin, he brought up against
the question, which he left not really answered,
of the actual Divine permission of sin in this
best world. But leaving apart his theory of
theodicy, as an ordered statement of the rationale of faith in God in His world his Optimism is the noblest in all philosophy.

The next noticeable attempt at a theodicy
much resembles the outward aspect of this
idea of the best possible world as a world with
sin in it. It came, however, not from the
Theodicée, but from extreme Calvinism as it
dwelt in the minds of Hopkins and Bellamy,
the 'friends of Jonathan Edwards. Hopkins
argues that this " must be the wisest and best
possible plan, containing all the possible good
that infinite wisdom and goodness could devise
and desire, and omnipotence execute." This
optimism goes on to crystallise itself into a
theory of theodicy as follows. " There is,
therefore, the greatest possible certainty, from
the divine perfections, that sin does exist just
in the manner and in that degree, and in every
instance of it, with all the attendants and con-

sequents of it which do or will take place,
agreeably to the dictates of Infinite Wisdom
and Goodness, as being necessary to accomplish the most wise and best end, the greatest
possible good of the universe." And Bellamy
adds, "Were there no particular instance in
which we could see the wisdom of God in the
permission of sin, yet from the perfections of
the Divine nature alone, we have such full
evidence that he must always act in the wisest
and best manner, as that we ought not in the
least to doubt it." There is perhaps a mathematical certainty and infallibility about this
which reminds one more of the "scientific
method" of our own religious thought than
of the largeness and humanity of Augustine
or Leibnitz. It is faith drawing up a legal
document and setting down the laws of the
universe in it. And faith, when it advocates
Divine permission of sin, and represents sin
as the "necessary" means of the greatest
good, turns rational optimism into a theory of
theodicy, and into a very untenable as well as
unappealing one. But in its birth this theory

was an expression of rational faith in the wisdom and goodness and power of God in face of sin.

There is a much better and saner optimism in the suggestion of Dr. N. W. Taylor of Yale, that it may be that sin is possible here because it is an unavoidable possibility in the best moral system. This is less like the rhetoric of Leibnitz about the best world being one with sin in it, than like the real idea of Leibnitz that the best world is one containing "morality" and hence the unavoidable possibility of sin. When this suggestion was made the basis of a theodicy at Andover, it failed to meet all the facts of the case and to solve the problem of sin in the world. But in the mind of its author the idea of sin as an unavoidable possibility in the best moral system was simply an expression of rational belief that this moral system, in which sin exists, may be the best. This is an unassailable optimism. For the burden of proof is upon those who would deny that this is the best moral system. Butler in his classic argument in the "Analogy" lays this

burden of proof upon them when he shows
that we have no ground but ignorance for
doubting the wise and good plan of God in
this world. And those who would deny the
goodness and power of God have a burden
which cannot be carried, for sin, which is no
more real than God, cannot be used to disprove
His existence. The true optimism which acknowledges sin because it is real, and acknowledges God because He is real, is the only honest
or rational attitude to take in regard to the
problem of sin and God.

This rational optimism cannot, however, be
taken as a solution of the problem. The problem may not have to be solved. The faith of
him who knows God may descend, like the
Angel Michael against the dragon, and easily
triumph by the touch of celestial temper over
sin's denial of God. But it is a problem which
is well worth removing, for at one time or another it troubles almost every mind. And to
solve it we need more than the rational faith
which sees both sin and God and sees God in
spite of sin. Sin's seeming denial of God

may have no real effectiveness, for God is as
real as sin, and His undeniable existence may
equally well be used to deny the existence of
sin.   But if we desire a solution of the problem of sin, it is not enough to let the visible
existence of God overcome sin's denial of Him.
We must not only overcome but must remove
sin's denial of Him, by showing that the existence of sin in His world is not inconsistent
with His goodness and power.   We cannot do
this by showing that His goodness and power
are so great and so clear in general that they
cannot be denied by sin's seeming denial.
That is rational optimism.   But we must show
that God's goodness and power are not questionable or uncertain in this particular case
where they are challenged by sin.   That will
be a rational solution.

Looking upon the problem itself in that
rational way, there is one hypothesis in regard
to the facts which is plainly out of the question.   It is incredible, though we believe that
God created His world, that God should be the
author of sin.   Such an hypothesis denies the

realities of the case, for it means either that
God is not God, holy and perfect, or that sin is
not sinful. We are thrown at once, then,
upon the only possible explanation. This sin,
which does not come from God, is not an im-
personal thing, an abstraction, a being by itself,
self-born and self-existent, roaming the world
alone. It is human beings who sin. When
we say that " sin defies God," we mean that
"sinners defy God." If sin is against God's
will, it is because those who sin are sinning
against God's will. Their wills are free
enough and independent enough to sin in spite
of God. No other hypothesis is possible unless we deny the reality of sin as moral evil.
Sin is not of God's will, and though we may
ascribe much to the devil, or, as evolutionists,
may demonise matter, sin is not something
with a will of its own outside of us. It
is the work or the working of man's
will. It is hardly necessary to refer to
consciousness, which declares in the soul,
" It is I who sin my sin, and I am able
to sin in spite of the will of God," or to

the consciousness speaking morally in our
conscience, which we can neither escape nor
drive out, and which tells us that we are
responsible for our sin. The evident logic of
the case runs in the same way. For only a
will can defy a will; a mere existence without
a will cannot. Human sin could not exist in
the face of the holy will of God if there were
not a will, a human will, in it. One may analyse further, as Leibnitz did, and say that
since will is the cause of existence, only a will
can give evil an existence; it cannot be God's
will which does this; therefore it must be man's
will. All this however is but analysis of the
simple and evident fact, with which consciousness agrees, that defiant sin is but the free
human will defying God.

In this free human will we have the explanation of the otherwise inconceivable fact that
sin exists in the world in spite of God. In
place of God and strange defiant sin, we have
God and defiant sinning souls. Sin reveals
itself in more personal form set over against
God. God must be good, and sin, in the soul,

is evil. God must be full of power, and sin
defies Him. The problem gathers itself into
the famous dilemma which troubled Lactan-
tius and other ancient philosophers, and gave
such joy to Voltaire, Bayle, and Hume: " Is
sin by God's consent? Then it denies His
goodness. Is it in spite of Him? Then it
denies His power." It is a natural dilemma,
and though we may not assent to its too easy
conclusion, we cannot get away from its alter-
nate question. Sin must be either " by God's
consent," or " in spite of Him." Whichever
view we take, we must reconcile it with both
His goodness and His power, which are the
two things which sin seems to deny, and the two
things to be shown in face of sin in a true
theodicy. For the question of the justice of
God, reflected in the word theodicy, is absorbed
in the question of His goodness, which sums
up His whole moral character. The question
of His wisdom also disappears in the question
of His goodness and power, for Divine goodness must be wise goodness, and Divine power
wise power. Everything else which may be

asked of God's character, nature or existence, in view of sin, is resolved into the question either of His goodness or of His power. The problem of theodicy is then clear before us. God must be good, but sin in His world is evil. God must be full of power, but sinners defy Him.

It is true that we cannot stake our belief in God upon the solution of the dilemma, for God is as real as the sin which is the basis of the question. But whichever side of the dilemma we take, it is necessary to vindicate both Divine goodness and Divine omnipotence at once, and not, as is sometimes done, to defend Divine goodness by holding that sin is in spite of God, and then to defend Divine omnipotence by showing that after all sin is by His consent. If we shift in this way, the dilemma will fell us, as it has felled others. If we say, for instance, that sin is in spite of God, we must show that it not only does not deny His goodness, but does not deny His power. This is really the side of the dilemma which, for every reason, we have from the

beginning chosen.   For instinct tells us naturally that sin is in spite of God.   In that lies
largely its heinousness and its moral quality.
We could add to this general instinct also the
witness of our conscience, which, if it tells us
anything of a superior moral Power, tells us
that that Power is wholly against our sins.
The very problem of sin is that sin seems to
be set against all that we must believe of God's
character and nature.   It is natural then, unless the contrary is proved, to assume that sin
is in spite of God.   And holding steadily that
sin is in spite of God, we must, in order to
reach a real theodicy, find that sin is no denial
either of His goodness or of His power.   If
that can be found, the theodicy is found.

IV

THE PROBLEM OF GOD'S GOODNESS

ONE thing is clear in regard to the goodness of God, and needs no argument. If sin is in spite of God, the fact that He does not prevent it is clearly no denial of His goodness in His government of the world. The question of His goodness is then rather a question of His creation of the soul which can sin, in spite of Him. For if sin is in spite of Him, His true moral responsibility is that He creates the soul whose sin He cannot prevent. It is inconceivable, certainly, that He creates it a sinful soul, or creates it with the seeds of sin in it. That would be, not a problem, but a flat denial of God. But the problem which sin raises in regard to God's goodness is that He creates the soul which can sin, and can sin in spite of Him.

We cannot evade this problem of God's

goodness in the creation of the soul by denying that the soul is His creation. For creation of the soul is the only theory of the origin
of the soul which is possible if we admit the
existence of God. Evolution, which seems to
many a theory of the origin of the soul, is,
except in its atheistic or agnostic form, a
theory simply of the mode of creation. In
fact, any other hypothesis than creation of
the soul directly denies God's existence. If
we declare that the soul is not His creation,
we have a dualism in the universe. We have
beings self-existent like Himself and defying
Him, or else created by some other defiant
self-existent being,—in either case an absolute denial of His omnipotence and hence of
His existence. Neither can we escape the
problem of the free soul as His creation by
affirming, as is so often done at the present
day, that the soul is not so directly a creation
of God that its defiance really defies Him,
because its will is really a part of His will
and even in its sin against God is uninten-
tionally carrying out His vaster will. For

this hypothesis, which if it did not claim to maintain the reality of sin would be pantheism, denies God, and, though it cannot destroy God, destroys itself; since if sinful creatures are really, and not rhetorically, a part of whatever God exists, then a sinless and holy God, the only God in whom we can believe, does not exist; and if He does not exist, human souls and wills cannot be in any way a part of Him. There is no escape, then, from the problem of the free soul as God's creation by denying that it is His creation. If sin exists and God exists, the soul which can sin, and whose sin He cannot prevent, must be His creation. This is the problem of sin and the goodness of God.

In facing the problem of God's goodness and His creation of the soul which can sin, the first thing to be done is to see just in what way sin is contrary to His goodness. This is easily seen.

Divine goodness seems to be challenged by sin in two different ways. Sin is a mystery in the universe of a good God first of all because it is evil, and defies His moral nature, His righteousness, or, we might best say, His holiness. And sin is also a mystery because it brings ruin and misery upon human beings, and so strikes at His love for men. Divine moral goodness, or holiness, and Divine love are the two aspects of Divine goodness which are concerned in sin, and of which we must ask the question concerning the defiant sinning soul as a Divine creation.

Is the creation of a moral being, with power of choice between good and evil, and consequent ability to sin, inconsistent with Divine holiness? The answer is contained in that very phrase, "a moral being." A moral being is one who, having the power of choice, is capable of moral goodness, or holiness. For holiness is more than mere sinlessness. The ox is sinless, but he is not holy. His being is a moral vacuum, as empty of moral good as it is of moral evil. Holiness is moral choice of good, that is, deliberate or instinctive, and habitual, choice of good by the free will, where evil might have been chosen. Where there is

no power to choose evil, the choice of good
means nothing, and is not really a choice. If
God then would create a being capable of holiness, he must create a moral being, capable of
choice. Such a being may have, and indeed,
if it comes from a holy Creator, must have,
a created tendency toward holiness, but it
must also have, to make holiness possible, the
power of choice, and hence the possibility of
sin. It cannot be questioned, then, that the
creation of a moral being, the only kind of
being who is capable of holiness, even though
capable also of sin, is consistent with Divine
holiness.

And beyond this truth, universally recognised, especially since Jonathan Edwards, we
may go so far as to say, for ourselves, that in
the highest sense the creation of a moral being
is the only creation which really involves
Creative holiness at all. For though the
Creator's benevolence may be active in the
creation of every living thing, and though
there may be a holy purpose in the creation
of the inanimate world, in so far as that world

is to influence moral beings, in the deepest
sense the only distinctively holy creation is
one in which holiness is the ultimate purpose,
as it is in the creation of a moral being.   And
we can see also that the creation of a moral
being is the only creation in which God could
take what we may call a receptively holy interest, as distinguished from His holy purpose for
the creation itself.   For the love and worship
of one moral being, who is free not to worship
and love, is worth more to Him than all the
inanimate or instinctive adoration of the universe.

It is beyond any question, then, that the
creation of a moral being, who is able to sin in
spite of God, but is above all able to be holy,
is consistent with Divine holiness, and is even
the only creation which could really reveal
Divine holiness to us.   And when we have
seen this we have seen the truth in regard to
Divine love and the creation of a moral being.
The creation of beings who have the Divine
prerogative of choice and the divine moral nature is certainly consistent with Divine love.

It is a far more loving creation than that of
beings who have not this part of the Divine
nature imparted to them. And it is surely a
work of Divine love, to give us the power, to
be holy by giving us the power of choice; it
is far more a work of love than, by cutting off
the alternative possibility of sinning, to cut
off all possibility of holiness and likeness to
God both now and in a future life.

And we may go again beyond this widely
recognised truth and say that while every
creative act may be benevolent, the creation of
a moral being is the only one which in the
deepest sense involves Divine love. For a
Divine loving Being, who delights in love,
must find the true delight which He has in
His creatures in the love of moral beings, who
are free not to love and whose love means
loving choice of Him. And in the same way
Divine love can bless and make blest in the
truest sense only those of its created beings
who can love as God loves, not by mere instinct, but with the soul, and who therefore
know what love is.

It is beyond question, then, that the creation of moral beings, which is consistent with Divine holiness, is consistent with Divine love, and seems in the highest sense the only kind of creation which could reveal Divine holiness and love. We are safe in affirming that the creation of a free soul, which, though it must have the power to sin, has the power and the tendency to be holy, and to love God, and to be blest by His holiness and love, is in every way consistent with Divine goodness, and is the highest creative revelation of that goodness. The defiant soul cannot be called a problem of Creative goodness. It is rather a witness to Creative goodness.

But, it may be asked, is the creation of a soul with power of choice a work of Divine holiness and love if the Creator foresees that soul sinning instead of becoming holy? Is the gift of moral freedom after all a good gift, when the Giver sees it used by the soul to efface its Maker's image and to destroy His purpose in its creation? The only answer to this question is the Redemption. So far we

have been in the region of natural religion,
though of natural religion latent in human
consciousness and reason until evoked by revealed truth. But we are brought here to the
central truth of revealed religion, the Redemption, as the only answer to the final question of sin and Divine goodness. We are
seeking, not to establish Christian truth, but
to find a rational and logical solution of this
problem of theodicy, one consistent with the
facts of the problem, that is, with the goodness and power of God and the sinfulness of
sin; and our search upon the grounds of reason has brought us to the point where the
Redemption is the only rational answer to the
question of Divine goodness. If we reject
the Redemption, not because it logically fails
to answer the question, but because of other
feelings or considerations outside of our problem, our search for a solution falls to the
ground. But if we desire an answer, consistent with the nature of God and the nature
of sin, to this further question of Divine goodness in creating a free soul, which, instead of

being holy, will actually sin, the Redemption
is the rational and consistent answer.

By the Redemption is meant God's saving
the soul from the sin into which it has fallen
and His giving to the soul eternal life, through
the incarnation, death and resurrection of His
Son Jesus Christ. This, which is not in any
way out of harmony with God's nature or with
the condition of sin in the soul, provides an
answer to the question of Divine goodness in
creating the soul with power of choice. For
if God, foreseeing sin, foresees also a redemption of the soul from sin and a final attainment
of holiness, there can be no question of the
reality of His good purpose in creating the
soul for holiness. We certainly might question the reality of a holy and loving purpose
in the creation of the soul if no soul was ever
to attain holiness. But if the Creator foresees human holiness attained at last through
the Redemption, His goodness is unquestioned
in creating a race of moral beings, the only
kind of beings capable at all of holiness. The
Redemption then gives complete reality to the

goodness of the Divine purpose in creating
the soul which now sins.

And beyond this it is also clear that Divine goodness in the creation of the soul shows
itself, in view of the Redemption, more glorious than if sin were not foreseen.   For while
the Creator only foresees sin, He not only
foresees, but makes, Redemption at His own
great cost.) And certainly the holiness of God
could not be shown so wonderfully in any
other way as in His putting even Himself, perfect as He is, under punishment, suffering and
death, that holiness might have its way in the
universe.   Certainly also Divine love could
not show itself so greatly in any other way as
in the gift of Itself for men.   Above and beyond the divine gift of moral freedom, beyond
an infinitude of blessings, beyond every other
gift of love, one thing yet remains,—God
Himself. Giving Himself in the Redemption,
He gives the one perfect and infinite gift of
love.) If God in creating the soul foresees
His purpose of holiness prevented by sin and
attained only through the Redemption, we see

His creation of the soul an infinitely holy and
loving thing. For we see the creation of the
soul a good creation when measured merely
by the holy human life which is the ultimate
purpose of the creation, but we see it infinitely
good when it is measured by the Divine life
which He sacrifices in the Redemption to carry
out that purpose. In the light of the Redemption, the creation, for holiness, of the soul
whose sin is foreseen, appears not only good,
but infinitely good.

We have found then in the good purpose
of the creation of the soul, enhanced and glori-
fied as that purpose is by the foreseen necessity of the Redemption, the rational and consistent solution of the problem of God's goodness and His creation of the soul which can
sin in spite of Him. For the gift of moral
freedom thus reveals itself as not an objection
but a witness to the goodness of Him who
made the soul. It was already clear that, if
God truly cannot prevent sin, its existence is
no denial of His goodness in His government
of the world. And there is now clearly no

denial of His goodness in the fact that He creates the soul which can sin in spite of Him. It is a positive and, in view of the Redemption, a measureless witness to His goodness, that He creates the soul which can be holy and which can sin. Sin is therefore no denial of the goodness of God.

V

THE PROBLEM OF GOD'S POWER

THE problem of the soul which sins in spite of God lies now in the fact that its sin is "in spite of God." It is now a problem not of Divine goodness, but of Divine power. And in meeting this question of Divine power we must be sure that we do not make it a question again of God's goodness by turning to the other position of the dilemma, that sin is by God's permission. We must show if we can that, while still in spite of Him, sin is no denial of His power. Neither can we do this by stating the unquestionable fact of God's omnipotence as an end of the discussion, for we must solve the question not by optimism, but by rational explanation of the facts of the problem itself as they have presented themselves to us.

With the question of God's goodness was a question of His creation of the soul, the

question of His power is a question of His
government of the world. And the ground
upon which the defiance of God by the sinning
soul seems to be a denial of God's power is of
course the fact that God's power must be
omnipotence. It must be infinite, limitless;
and the sinning soul by its defiance seems to
set a limit to it in His government of the
world. It is again the dilemma upon one
side or the other of which all the real theories
of theodicy range themselves. "Is sin by
God's consent, and does He limit His own
exercise of power in order to permit sin?
Then His goodness cannot be infinite." And
certainly those theories which hold that sin is
by God's consent must try to show that such
consent does not deny God's perfect goodness.
"Or is sin in spite of God?" For every reason of human consciousness and of God's nature, we have held that sin is in spite of God.
"Then," says the dilemma, "the sinning soul
limits His power, and His power cannot be
infinite." Holding then that sin is in spite of
God, we find sin a problem not of Divine

goodness, but of Divine power in the world. But though it is incredible to the human heart that sin should be by God's permission, and almost as strange that anyone should place Divine goodness in doubt rather than Divine omnipotence, we have the strange fact that nearly all the best known theories of theodicy meet this question of God's power in His world by declaring that sin is by Divine permission. In this way they dispose of the denial of His power, but they must take up, and do take up, the superhuman task of reconciling this permission with Divine goodness. We have therefore these theories of "permission of sin," which we must briefly consider, since they are among the leading theories of theodicy.

How can "permission of sin" be harmonized with the goodness of God? No one, indeed, among saner thinkers, has said that God actually approves of sin, for that is a thing inconceivable upon any true view of the reality of God and sin. But the basis of these theories is the idea that while sin itself is hateful to

God, He permits it for the sake of other and higher things. Or, if we would have this idea in its most definite form, it is that God permits sin, evil in itself, as a means of greater good than could have been brought to pass without it.   This idea appears first in the *Theodicée* of Leibnitz, where he has drawn out with much eloquence the thesis that sin is permitted by Divine goodness because it makes possible the " best possible world.". Evil, he says, is thus a means of good, for the world needs both good and evil.   Light needs shadow, and heat needs cold, in order to make possible by contrast an enhanced and vivid existence of light and heat, and so good needs evil, for there cannot really be good without its opposite.   It is somewhat of a surprise, then, to find Leibnitz, on his descent to sober argument, explaining that he means that sin is a necessity, or at least that the possibility of sin is a necessity, in a world of moral agents, which is the best kind of a world. Sin is, according to Leibnitz, a necessary means of good only to this extent, that the possibility of

sin, being inherent in moral freedom, is unavoidable in a moral world.   For this existence of a moral world requires the existence
of moral beings, who by their Divinely-given
nature are able to sin in spite of God.   And
from this Leibnitz argues that though sin is in
spite of God, there is no denial of God's power
in the fact that He cannot coerce the soul,
since the limitation of His power lies in this
uncoercible nature of free will.   It is evident
upon a very slight analysis, then, that Leibnitz regards sin as being in spite of God, and
that his theodicy, though it may appear so at
first sight, is not one of Divine permission of
sin.

It is in Puritan New England, in the school,
if we may call it so, of Jonathan Edwards
that the theory of sin as the necessary means
of the greatest good first arises in any serious-
ness. The extreme Calvinism of Hopkins
and Bellamy, in which they ran not only beyond Calvin, but beyond Edwards, beheld all
things, even sin itself, as planned and carried
out by the sovereign Will of God for a su-

preme purpose, which was the greatest or highest good.   And if sin is thus willed by the Will of God, it must be because sin is a necessary means of the highest good.   Even in a time when thinkers followed logic to conclusions, as we seldom do now, and among those who carried their doctrine of Divine Sovereignty to the point of complete fatalism, very few were drawn by this doctrine of a direct Divine purpose in sin.   But the idea found wider favour in the modified theory that though man's will, and not God's, is the source of sin, God permits man to sin because sin is the necessary means of the greatest good. Yet even in this modified form the idea cannot commend itself to a rational or reverent mind.   It is too much of a Divine doing of evil that good may come, or an apotheosis of the Jesuitical creed that the end justifies the means. The idea, even with a glamour of logic about it, is of itself inconceivable.   And there is good reason for our instinctive antipathy to that idea, for even in this form of mere "permission of sin as a necessary means of

the greatest good" there lurks the danger
which lay in the view of a direct Divine purpose in sin.   The danger, the fatal defect, is
this, that if sin is the necessary means of the
greatest good, then God, in planning the
greatest good, must make sin a certainty, either
by implanting sin in the souls whom He creates, or by leading them inevitably into sin, in
order to make the greatest good inevitable.
And on the other hand there is no justification
for suggesting a Divine permission of sin as a
means to the Divine end unless it is the necessary means.   This view, therefore, of Divine
permission of sin as the necessary means of
the greatest good throws the responsibility for
sin, and in a very real sense the authorship of
sin, upon God.   There is nothing in the idea
to bring us to belief in permission of sin.

Nevertheless when we come to see what the
thought of the present day can do with the
dilemma, we find this same idea in a new and
philosophical dress, as a part, and a vital part,
of the theory called evolution.   Strictly speaking, the theory of evolution has no use for Di-

vine permission of sin. The science of Darwin and the philosophy of Spencer neither assumed nor desired to explain the universe from a theistic point of view. But that kind of evolutionary theory which has abandoned Darwin and Spencer, and has become theistic and even religious, does claim to be a philosophy of the work of God in His universe, or at least in His world. And as a theory of the world it meets at once the great question of the existence of sin in the world. But here, at the one and supreme problem which as a world-theory it has to solve, it must be said that the evolutionary theory fails. For it offers as its only real solution of the problem the old idea of sin as the means of the greatest good.

For according to this theory of evolution the world is now in the midst of a vast unfolding and upward-growing process, the motive power of which is the infinite Will of God, and the goal of which is the perfection of the race, or the highest good of the world, or some far-off divine event. It is in many ways an inspiring conception of the Divine plan of the world. But in any plan of the world the great fact which most needs explanation is the fact of sin. And the presence of sin cannot be explained merely by the supposition, or by the proof, if we could prove it, that the race is being brought by a Divine process out of sin into a perfect life, for the presence of sin at the present time in this process is what requires solution.

The same thing applies to all theodicies which have universal salvation or restoration of souls for their basis, as, for instance, the eloquent Theodicy of George A. Gordon ("Immortality and the New Theodicy"). To say, even if it could be said with truth, that all souls may be saved from sin, does not touch the problem of theodicy.

If we ask for an explanation of the presence of sin in the world during this process, we shall get it somewhat in this wise: that sin unavoidably arises from the material nature out of which the race is growing. For God's method of creating the perfect race, the theory runs, is by evolving it, or causing it to evolve, out of a material, earthy nature, up into the life of the spirit. And during the process this material nature, this clinging earthiness, necessarily and inevitably hinders the soul in its progress and causes it to sin. Sin, therefore, which arises from the necessities of this material beginning or investiture of the race, is a necessary part of the evolution of the race, and since it is unavoidable, its existence is not in any way to be made a charge against God's goodness. But, we may ask, is the existence of sin in this process actually in spite of God? Is it a radical defect and break in the process, by which sin has gotten the better of the Divine Will? For if that is so, there is very little left of the evolutionary plan and its certain outcome. But the evolutionist would explain to us that, though the soul sins directly against God, nevertheless God's Will overrules and includes in its vast process and purpose all these defiant human wills, and is using even their sin, which they think is wholly in spite of Him, as a part of His evolution of the

race. God refrains from crushing out sin,
because it is a necessary element in His
method of evolving a perfect race from animalism. There are some evolutionists, represented very well by John Fiske, who declare
that sin is not only a necessary element in the
Divine method of evolving the race from
earthiness, but that sin is actually the essential
thing in the process. John Fiske, for instance,
represents sin as necessary to spiritual growth,
and as one of the Divine agencies in the up-
lifting of the race. He quotes Leibnitz, to
the effect that there can be no morality without the possibility of sin, and going himself
beyond this sees no morality possible without
actual sin. He, and those whom he represents, look upon sin as a spur or stimulus to
the soul, as a contrast which makes the good
more desired by the soul, and as an occasion
for moral and spiritual choice. At this point
sin becomes so wholly a means of good that
it really ceases to be evil. The evolutionist
passes into practical denial of the reality of
sin, and beholds " every fall as a fall upward,"

and sees the progress of the race beginning
with Adam's sin. This denial of the reality
of sin is the natural outcome of the evolutionary view of sin as a means of the highest
good. Every paradox tends to dissolve into
unreality, and the paradox of sin as a means
of good is no exception. For sin, as a means
of good, becomes good in itself, not only in the
rhapsodic logic of Emerson or the genial as-
sumptions of John Fiske, but in the thought
of every evolutionist who follows his own
theory to its end.

Perhaps it is hardly fair to let the logical
conclusion of evolution in regard to sin crowd
out the witness of the moderate evolutionist,
who is a follower of revealed religion as well
as of evolution, and who does not go with
evolution to its panegyric on sin as a positive
good. His view of the case is that God is
limiting His exercise of power in order to let
the soul sin, simply because sin, though it is
not pleasing to Him, is a necessity in the evolution of the perfect race from animalism. This
is a theory deserving the name of a theodicy,

and is the only theory of theodicy which evolutionary thought can honestly propose. For
the hypothesis that sin is really a good is not
a solution but an evasion of the problem. And
the hypothesis that sin, being evil, is in the
evolutionary process entirely in spite of God
is not a theory of theodicy, for it merely states
the problem. Moreover, this opinion, that sin
is wholly in spite of God, while it is a safe and
sane attitude in general, is a fatal attitude for
the evolutionist. The believer in a fallen race
and in a world not going wholly according
to God's plan may hold that sin is in spite of
God, but the evolutionist, who sees the present
order of things as a carrying out of God's
great plan, cannot hold that so great a part of
this order as sin is can be in spite of God.
The only theodicy which the evolutionary
philosophy can offer is this of the modern
school, that God permits sin because sin is a
necessity in the evolution of a perfect race
from earthiness. This is not a new theodicy,
it is true, for it is but the old idea, newly-drest,
of Hopkins and Bellamy, that sin is permitted

as the necessary means of the greatest good. We have but to put the perfecting of the race or the far-off divine event in place of the greatest good. Nor should it be really surprising that the evolutionist, who thinks of Calvin a little as Calvin thought of the devil, should have come to the extreme conclusion of Calvinism, far beyond Calvin's own logic. For hyper-Calvinism and Evolution are much at one. Both behold the world under the spell of one great idea. The all-embracing, overriding Will of God, the great Idea of Evolution, is but the Divine Sovereignty which was the sole idea of extreme Calvinism. And the survival of the fittest, with its destruction of the unfit, is but Election writ in terms mechanical and merciless. As for this mutual idea of Divine permission of sin as the necessary means of the greatest good, it is open to the same fatal objection as in its Calvinistic days. If sin is not the necessary means, there is no excuse for imagining its use as the means; and if it is the necessary means, it makes God necessarily the planner and author

of sin. And while the older theory failed because by implication it made sin inevitable,
the evolutionary theory openly shows God as
making sin inevitable by putting the soul in an
environment in which, according to the evolutionary view, it not only can sin, but must sin.
The evolutionary theory of God's work in the
world, when it meets the one great problem
which such a theory has to solve, needs only
to declare itself in order to be discredited. It
has certainly done nothing to lead us to that
naturally inconceivable view that sin is by
God's consent.

But there is a much simpler theory of permission of sin than these which we have just
discussed, and it is one held more or less for-
mally by many who think upon this problem.
This theory is that God, who has created the
free soul for a holy purpose, limits His own
exercise of power in order to let the free soul
sin. For He could not directly prevent the
soul's sinning without destroying its moral
freedom, with its possibility and purpose of
holiness. God's holy and loving purpose in

creating a moral being like the soul is held in
this theory to justify and explain Divine permission of sin. This idea is certainly founded
on primary facts, not on disputable theories
of the universe, and it reduces the hypothesis
of permission of sin to its simplest terms. Nor
does it make sin inevitable, as do the theories
of sin as the necessary means of greatest good.
But it has still the superhuman task of making
credible the inconceivable idea that the holy
God should directly permit sin, and to this
task it brings nothing of very great force. Its
facts have weight enough, but no momentum
in this direction. The final holiness of the soul
made sure by the Redemption may be sufficient
reason for the creation of the soul by a good
God, but it is certainly not reason enough for
a Divine permission of sin. It is not at all to
the point to prove, as Julius Müller does in his
great work on "The Christian Doctrine of
Sin," that in the abstract it is loving in Divine
power to limit itself when there is occasion,
since such limitation is akin to self-sacrifice,
or as De Pressensé does, that "Divine liberty

can certainly put limits on itself, can even
assert itself by voluntarily accepting the limitation imposed by the created liberty of which
it is itself the source." The question is not
whether God can limit Himself, nor whether
He can prove His own liberty by doing so, but
whether He can limit Himself to allow sin,
and whether His own liberty will let Him allow sin. And if Self-limitation to allow sin
were a sacrifice, what would it sacrifice? As
a self-sacrifice it would sacrifice Divine holiness, which is inconceivable, and secondly it
would sacrifice, not self, but the souls whom
it permitted to sin, which is not self-sacrifice
at all. The holy and loving purpose of God
in creating the soul makes it more inconceivable than ever, in fact, that He should permit
sin to ruin the soul and affront Him in it. If
His purpose in the soul were merely negative,
it might have no bearing upon the question
of permission of sin. But if His purpose for
the soul is one of holiness and love, that attitude toward the soul renders Divine permission of unholiness and ruin in the soul more

inconceivable than ever, unless sin is the
necessary means of the final holiness of the
soul; and that, we have seen, is incredible, because it would make God necessarily the
author of sin.   We may as well admit, therefore, that Divine self-limitation to permit sin
is inconceivable. The sooner we do so, also,
and admit that sin is wholly in spite of God,
the sooner we shall make theology credible to
the popular mind, which troubles itself but
little about any question of God's power, but
very greatly about any question of His goodness, and has long found in the idea that God
permits sin the great stumbling-block of theology.   For there is nothing which can make
conceivable a direct withholding of Divine
power for the sake of sin.   The Redemption
makes the creation of a free soul, which can
sin and will sin, a holy and loving act, but even
the Redemption could not make Divine self-
limitation to let the soul sin a holy and loving
act.

It is often represented, however, that, although we cannot say that the Redemption

could make permission of sin a holy and loving act, nevertheless it does give us an explanation of Divine permission of sin. For the Redemption, which would not have taken place if there were no sin, is in its glory of love the supreme good in the universe. It is not probable, indeed, that anybody conceives that God causes sin in order to make the Redemption possible, but it seems to many thinkers that the wondrous character of the Atonement which is occasioned by sin overcomes the inconceivability of God's permitting sin. For theological thinkers, of older and newer schools alike, perceive that sin gave occasion for the supreme display of Divine love in the incarnation, sufferings and death of Jesus Christ. And those who hold to moderate Calvinism, who are doubtless in the great majority, would add that not only was Divine love revealed in the Atonement as in no other way, but that holiness and justice were revealed as in no other way, and that mercy and compassion, and self-sacrifice, would not have been revealed at all without it. And because

of this a large number, and among them some
of the noblest and most reverent thinkers, are
inclined to hold that the Atonement in its glory
of love and holiness must make permission of
the· sin which occasions the Atonement conceivable in a holy and loving God.

This is by far the best of all theories of permission of sin, for certainly if anything could
outweigh the inconceivability of Divine permission of sin, the Divine Atonement could.
And this theory has to the believer in revealed
religion the great thing in its favour that it is
Scriptural.   But while the Atonement or Redemption is Scriptural, the idea of its making
possible the permission of sin is a deduction
from the Scripture facts.   For the most which
we can draw from the Scriptures in this connection is that because He has a Redemption
for them God does not destroy at once the
whole sinful race of men and so blot sin from
the cleansed universe.   But to say that God
refrains from destroying sinners is not the
same as saying that He limits Himself to let
them become sinners.   God may bear patiently

with sinners in order to save them, but shall
He also let them become sinners in order to
save them? And do the glory and the love
revealed in saving them make it credible that
He should directly permit them to sin? Does
the Redemption make Divine permission of
sin conceivable? Now, when we stop to consider the relation of the Redemption to sin, we
see that it is very far from making such a thing
conceivable. For the Redemption shows sin
as worse than we should ever have known it
to be. For it is because sin is evil, and strikes
at God's holiness, and ruins those whom He
loves, that it calls for the Redemption. In the
Redemption, then, we see for the first time
some real measure, the only wholly Divine measure, of the greatness of sin. The unholiness
of sin is supremely revealed in God's sacrifice
of His very self to satisfy the needs of holiness
because of sin. And the harmfulness of sin
to those whom He loves is supremely revealed
in His giving Himself to save them from its
results. The Atonement, therefore, makes it
more than ever inconceivable that the holy and

loving God should directly permit so immeasurable an evil. For the Atonement not only reveals the whole evil of sin, but it shows God as set with His whole nature and character, yes, and with His life, and His very death, against sin. If Divine permission of sin is inconceivable already, we can find it only more inconceivable, if that were possible, in the light of the Atonement. If it be true that human suffering because of sin is God's protest against sin,—and there is every reason to believe it true—certainly His own suffering because of sin, and for the destruction of sin, is God's infinite protest against sin.

These arguments for Divine permission of sin have been from the beginning doomed to failure. For they propose something inconceivable to human minds, which on the one side feel unalterably that a perfectly good Ruler cannot withhold His own power in order to permit sin, and on the other feel too strongly the witness of their own conscience that their sin is really, and not apparently, against God. It must be a very great weight of argument which could reverse this feeling. But far from reversing it, these arguments have all alike ended by making the idea of Divine permission of sin more inconceivable than before.   And the reason is that all facts tell against such a primary impossibility, and the largest facts, therefore, such as God's desire for the greatest good, or His plan for a perfect race, or His holy creative purpose in the soul, or the Atonement, which these theories have laid hold of, tell most largely against the inconceivable idea.   Sin as the " necessary means of the greatest good " would involve God as the author of sin. Evolution would directly reveal God as the author of sin.   God's holy creative purpose in the soul makes voluntary permission of unholiness in the soul more inconceivable than ever. The Atonement, God's infinite protest against sin, renders " Divine permission of sin " most inconceivable of all.

We must recognise, then, as beyond question the fact that sin is in spite of God.   For these theories of permission of sin have only

made permission of sin more incredible than
ever. We must hold that the soul's defiance
of God is as real as it seems to the soul. We
must believe our consciousness, our conscience,
and God's protest in natural evil, when they
tell us that sin is in spite of God. These
theories have led us no nearer to a theodicy,
except as we have seen yet more clearly that
sin is in spite of God, that He is unalterably
set against it, and that, if it is in spite of God,
its existence is no denial of His perfect goodness in His government of the world. The
real problem of His goodness is that He creates the soul which can so sin in spite of Him.
And in regard to this we have found that sin
is no denial of His goodness in creating the
soul, but is even a witness to His goodness in
making the soul able to sin and consequently
able to be holy. The problem is still,
therefore, a problem of His power, which must
be omnipotence, and which is defied by sin.

VI

THE POWER OF GOD, AND THE THEODICY

THE question of defiant sin, therefore, is now a question not of God's goodness, but of His power. If sin is in spite of God, does not the soul limit His power, and is His power then omnipotence? How shall we reconcile this defiance with His omnipotence? We cannot do it at the expense of His goodness, by falling back upon the idea of some Divine permission or use of sin. Since, then, He cannot righteously restrain the exercise of His own power in order to permit the soul to sin, what does restrain His righteous power in this case? Does the soul do it? That is as inconceivable, we must admit, as is Divine self-limitation to permit sin, for while that denies His goodness, this limitation by the soul denies His omnipotence. But if sin is in spite of Him and He does not re-

strain His own power, nor does the soul restrain Him, what does restrain His power?

We have, to help us at the beginning of this
problem, a few theories, already partly familiar
to us, which form the nearest approach which
has been made to a true theory of theodicy.
First in these attempts, as in nearly every line
of thought upon this problem, stands the work
of Leibnitz. For we come now at last to the
true logic, often obscured, and often abandoned by Leibnitz himself, of the *Theodicée*.
It is, in brief, that God has not prevented evil
because evil is unavoidable in the best possible world. For the best possible world is
one containing morality, or free moral agents,
and in such a world sin is an unavoidable possibility. But Leibnitz clearly does not mean,
as he sometimes seems to mean, that God limits
Himself in order to let moral agents exist and
sin. For he explains that neither does God
limit Himself to permit sin, nor does sin limit
Him and deny His omnipotence, but that it is
the uncoercible, uncontradictable nature of a
moral being which prevents His using His

omnipotence against sin. And therefore, while sin is wholly in spite of God, it is not a limitation of omnipotence by sin, but Divine rational inability to contradict the soul's nature, which keeps Him from directly preventing sin.

And before we consider this theory, we may set beside it the suggestion of Dr. N. W. Taylor of New Haven, that God may have refrained from directly preventing sin because, though He hates it, it cannot be prevented in the best moral system. This in itself is but a suggestion, refreshing in its undogmatic tone, and yet at the most only an affirmation of faith that this is the best moral system. But this suggestion was made a theory at Andover, to the same general purpose as the idea of Leibnitz. In this constructive form the theory was that God has not prevented sin because He cannot in a moral system—that is, not only that He cannot in the best moral system, but that He cannot in any moral system. For a moral system is one containing free agents whose very nature is uncontradictable and uncoercible. It is not, therefore, Divine choice nor yet Divine impotence which keeps God from directly preventing sin, but only Divine inability to contradict the uncontradict- able.

And beside these two theories may be set a third, which reduces them to the simplest terms. It is, that for God to coerce the soul in the action of its free nature would be a "contradiction," and that even God cannot work a contradiction, "for a contradiction is not an object of power."

Now it is true that God, who must be a rational Being, cannot contradict that which is rationally uncontradictable by Him. And it is true that He cannot work a true contra- diction, that is, a contradiction of Himself. Such a contradiction is clearly impossible to omnipotence. These theories of theodicy have gone beyond all others, therefore, in the fact that they have grasped the principle upon which the dilemma must be solved. If the impossibility of God's coercing the soul lies in God's own rational and consistent nature, which cannot contradict itself, the dilemma is solved. For it is no denial of His omnipotence that He cannot work a contradiction of Himself, and, as an impossibility, it is no denial of His goodness that He does not do it. The true theodicy, however, must not only recognise this principle as the only way to a solution of the dilemma, but it must also show just how Divine coercion of the soul would be a true " contradiction," a contradiction of God by Himself.

One thing is plainly true in the statement that for God to coerce the free soul in its action would be for Him to work a contradiction, and that is that there would be a contradiction of the free soul's nature. This is also what the theories of Leibnitz and of a "moral system" declare, that the coercion of the soul would be a complete contradiction of its nature. And it is beyond question that the soul is in its very nature free and uncoercible. But whether this incoercibility of the soul belongs only to the soul's nature, or has power also over God's nature, is another question. The true answer to this will be the true theodicy. What is this uncontradictable nature of the free soul or of a moral system? Is it such that the soul's nature is as strong as God, and there- fore uncontradictable by Him, and that it can of its own power defy and restrain His power? That would be no solution of the dilemma, for it would deny God's omnipotence; it can hardly, therefore, be what these theories mean. What then is their answer to the question: how is coercion of the free soul a contradiction of God by Himself?

Their answer, implied or expressed, is that the freedom and incoercibility of the soul, be- ing the soul's very nature, belongs to the na- ture of things, and that God cannot contradict the laws of the nature of things, because they are grounded in His own rational nature. He cannot contradict these laws, then, either to make two and two equal more than four, or to make the sum of the angles of a triangle equal less than two right angles, or, it is said, to coerce a free soul's action. Now it may not be absolutely certain that numerical and geometrical laws lie in God's nature, that they are not created, and not within His power to change. But if they are, there is still the main question, whether the free nature of the soul belongs, as they do, to the nature of things. Holding, as doubtless we must, that these laws lie in God's nature and are immutable, there is the great and radical difference between them and the sinning soul, that they are in harmony with God's power and nature, while the sinning soul is defiant of His power and nature. And granting that they lie in God's nature, and are not merely created, there is an absolute difference between them and the sinning soul, in the fact that the freedom of the soul is a created thing. It is not at all, like mathematical axioms, a law of God, and hence of the nature of things, but is only a law of the soul, which is itself, to all but the pantheist, a creation, not a part of God's nature. The freedom of the soul belongs then, not to the nature of God, but only to the nature of the soul. It cannot therefore be said on this ground that Divine coercion of the soul would be a contradiction of God's own nature by Himself. The true theodicy must lie beyond these and all other theories, and it is for us to find it.

How then would there be a contradiction of God by Himself, if He were to coerce the soul and so prevent sin? What would it really mean, that He should contradict the uncontradictable nature of the soul, uncontradictable perhaps by all save omnipotence? Simply this, that the nature of the soul, as a free and uncontradictable nature, would be destroyed. Divine coercion and contradiction of the free soul would be Divine destruction of the free and uncontradictable soul. This, which is a truth long evident to all who believe in the free soul, is the root of the matter in regard to Divine prevention of sin. Yet in itself it is not an answer to the question of theodicy. For how would destruction of the soul's free nature be a contradiction of God by Himself? If one says that God, in His desire for "morality," or a "moral system," or in His love for "moral beings," must permit

sin because He cannot directly prevent it without destroying these, one simply returns to
" permission of sin," with its denial of Divine
goodness.   Or if, to avoid the idea of voluntary permission of sin, we say that the destruction of the free soul would be a contradiction
of God by Himself, because something in His
nature absolutely requires the existence of free
souls, or of a moral system, or of a world
with morality in it, the difficulty is not
overcome.   For if this were true, it would
indicate, not that God could not coerce the soul
and destroy these things, but that He permits
its sin in order to satisfy the demand of His
nature for these things, and this is incredible.
Moreover, we know of nothing at all to prove
such a demand in His nature, and if we did,
it would by no means prove, or even indicate,
that this particular system or these particular
souls which have sin in them are necessary to
 His nature.   The self-contradiction of God,
in this destroying of the soul, is yet to be
found.   Why cannot God at once destroy this
free soul which is not a part of Him,

but only a creation, and which cannot be coerced in its sin without being destroyed? We have seen that as Ruler of the world the rational and consistent thing for Him to do would be to prevent sin even by destroying the soul, and it is His not preventing sin which has led men to doubt Him as Ruler of the world. Can it be because He created the soul that He cannot rationally and consistently destroy it? There seems some reason in the idea. For His relation as Creator is His primary relation to the soul, and as Creator of the soul He stands, not over against the defiant soul, as the soul causes Him to stand as Ruler of the world, but, as it were, back of the soul and its free nature. But the mere fact that God is Creator is not a solution of the problem, and does not make it a self-contradiction for Him to destroy the soul. The fact that God has created a thing does not bind Him not to destroy it. It has been often said, indeed, that "God cannot both create and destroy." But the problem cannot be met, nor God's self-consistency involved, by the bare enunciation of the fact that He is the Creator. The self-consistency of God as Creator of the soul, if in some way His coercing and destroying the soul would contradict Him as Creator, would be a clear and plain solution of the problem; but we must go beyond the mere fact of His creating the soul, to find this solution. For it is an absurdity to say that merely because God creates a thing He cannot consistently destroy it. If it were true, He could never destroy anything. It would deny in Him not only omnipotence, but any real power at all in His world. And it is plainly not true that as a general principle God cannot destroy what He has created. He can often do it, and it is neither self-contradictory nor irrational. Some things even fulfil the purpose of their creation by being destroyed, and some may be destroyed when they have fulfilled their purpose. The inconsistency and contradiction in this destroying of the soul which He has created is therefore yet to be found, and found in a hitherto untrodden path.

The first thing which appears in that path

is that God's coercing and destroying the free soul would be very different from His destroying other things which He had created. Some things, we have said, fulfil their purpose by being destroyed, and some may be destroyed with their purpose already sufficiently fulfilled. But destroying the soul, far from fulfilling this purpose in creating the soul, or from leaving that purpose already fulfilled, would break off and contradict His purpose of holiness and love in creating the soul. It would be working at cross-purposes with Himself. And this is impossible to a self-consistent Being. The question about the soul then is this: Can God, when He has created a thing with a great and distinct purpose, rationally and consistently destroy that creation with the purpose wholly unaccomplished? Can He, creating moral beings, as we know, with a great purpose, rationally and self-consistently destroy those beings with His purpose wholly unaccomplished in them? The soul may act at cross-purposes with Him, and this is its sin; but can He so act at cross-purposes with Him-

self? The soul may by its sin be inconsistent
with His purpose; but can He be inconsistent
with His own purpose? The soul may try to
contradict the purpose and working of His
power in its creation, and herein lies the soul's
sin; but can He do so Himself? Plainly He
cannot. He cannot consistently or rationally
make His own creative purpose meaningless
and irrational. He cannot contradict Himself, and join with the soul in its sinful re-
volt against His work and purpose. It would
be to sin against His own Divine nature, as
the soul sins against Him. This is but rational self-consistency. It is a very different
thing from being unable, merely because He
created the soul, to coerce and destroy the soul.
It is inability to work at cross-purposes with
Himself. Neither is it merely that having
once given the soul a free nature He cannot
do anything inconsistent with that nature
which he has created. The freedom of the
soul does not lie in His nature, with which
alone He cannot be inconsistent, as His own
unity of purpose and of working does. Nor

is it a mere voluntary carrying out of His purpose because it is a good purpose.   Whatever
His purpose in creating free souls, though we
see it a good as well as a great one, it is but
rational self-consistency which must keep Him,
by the law of His nature, from breaking and
contradicting that purpose.   It is true that the
same self-consistency might require that He
should carry out His holy purpose in spite of
the soul's sinning, or else that He should not
create at all, and in this is a profound reason
of the Atonement.   But apart from this, if
He is the Creator, who has made the soul with
a great purpose, He cannot in rational self-
consistency coerce and destroy the free soul, to
prevent sin.   This is not voluntary self-
restraint or self-limitation on the part of God
to permit sin, even with a good purpose.
Neither is it restraint or limitation by the soul
or its nature.   It is but the inability of omnipotence to contradict itself.   It is but Divine self-
consistency and self-unity.   It passes through
the dilemma.   Sin is not by God's consent;
He would prevent it if He could, and protests

against it in natural evil; and His goodness remains unquestioned. And yet sin, though it is in spite of Him and He is unalterably set against it in His creature the soul, is no denial of His omnipotence, for it is His Creative self-consistency, which He could not break rationally or without sin against His highest nature, which must restrain Him in the case of the sinning soul. Such self-consistency and self-unity is the very principle of the being of God. It is in the highest sense the " wholeness," or holiness, which is, not an attribute, like His love, His righteousness, or His power, but the very nature itself, of God.

Since sin is in spite of God, there is no denial of His goodness in the fact that He does not prevent it. And it is no denial of His goodness that He creates the soul whose sin He cannot prevent. For in the light of His holy and loving creative purpose, and of the Redemption, the creation of a soul which can sin, and does sin, and whose sin He cannot prevent, is a witness to His goodness. And on the other hand we have seen that it is no denial of His power that He cannot prevent sin, for even omnipotence cannot contradict itself, and rational self-consistency must restrain Him in the case of the sinning soul. Sin, being in spite of God, is then no denial either of God's goodness or of God's power.

This is all that is needed to make the true theodicy. We need but to find, as we have found, that sin is no denial of God. And in finding that it is no denial of His goodness or His power, we have found that it is no denial at all of Him. For the dilemma of Divine goodness and power is the only real question propounded by sin. All other questions which sin occasions in regard to God gather themselves up in that. The question, for instance, reflected in the word theodicy, of Divine justice and the injustice in the world, is simply a question of the defiance of a just and good God by unjust sin with its acts and consequences. It is a question of defiant sin and God. And defiant sin is the problem in natural evil, which flows from sin, and punishes sin, and vindicates the universe against sin, and reveals God set over against sin. Natural evil, flowing from sin, and occasioned by sin, is no denial of God if sin is not a denial of Him. And now we see that defiant sin itself is no denial of either God's goodness or God's power. The most we could admit was that it was a seeming denial, for God is as real as the sin which would seem to deny Him. But now we see that it is not even a seeming denial, for it is no denial of His power that He does not prevent sin, if as Creator He is rationally withheld from doing it. And it is no denial of His goodness that He with holy and loving purpose and in view of the Redemption creates the soul whose sin He cannot prevent. The theodicy is therefore complete.

VII

THE CREATIVE PRINCIPLE

THERE remains, however, another question. Is it not possible to find sin not only no denial of God, but even a positive witness to God? For there are many who have never believed that sin really denied God, who have nevertheless felt vague misgivings and doubts because of sin. There are many for whom sin has not shut off the sight of God, but to whom it has obscured Him. If sin could be found not only no denial of God, but even a positive witness to God, this would blot out that cloud upon the blaze of His existence. For the mind, when all else is a witness to God, is perplexed by this human sin which seems not to be a witness.

Sin is, as we have seen, a witness to God's goodness in the creation of the soul for holiness. But in regard to Divine power, though sin does not deny Divine power, it does not appear as a witness to it. If it did, it would meet that vague doubt whether, though His consistency as Creator removes sin's dilemma and denial of God, we can clearly see God at all as the Creator of such a soul,—a soul which can take advantage of Creative consistency to defy Divine power. It is a doubt whether we can really see God's power acting in the creation of the soul which can defy, even though it cannot deny, Divine power. All other things, the movement and balance of the heavens, the long ages of geology, the marvels of the earth, the detail of plant and animal life, the courses of history, are witnesses to Divine power back of them. The soul alone, which receives all this testimony, by its defiance seems not to set forth but to obscure Divine power. It is a less tangible question, and yet a more fundamental one, as to the existence of Divine power, than was the question of the dilemma. For that, though it denied, only denied that Divine power over the soul could be omnipotence, while this, though it only questions or doubts, questions or doubts any Divine power at all back of the defiant soul.   While all that can be demanded in the true theodicy is that it should show that sin does not deny God, yet if sin could be shown as a positive witness to God, to His power, as it is already to His goodness, this revelation would be of yet greater service both to the believer in God and to the unbeliever, by removing that vaguer but more fundamental doubt in regard to His existence.   Can human sin be found such a witness to God?   We can already see plainly His goodness in sin; can we see plainly His power? His goodness appears even in the soul's sin; does His power equally appear even in the soul's defiance?   To find whether it does we must follow yet further an untrodden path.

The paradox, that, where all else reveals God's power, man by his defiance should obscure God's power, is heightened when we remember that man seems in every other way to be the greatest creation of God's power known to us.

The Scripture closes the creation, which began with "Let there be Light," with the climax that " God made man in His own image." Even in the evolutionary view of the ages, man is the goal of the creative work. Philosophers and poets have shown that they regarded man as the greatest work of God known to us, by making him the subject of their epic and their drama, their histories and romances, and the region and matter of their philosophy. The attitude of philosophy was well summed up, if one takes " the world " to mean the created world, by the recent philosopher who liked to say, " In the world there is nothing great but man; in man there is nothing great but mind," that is, " but the soul of man." And yet the soul of man, which in other respects seems the highest work of God, seems by its attitude towards Him, by its defiance in sin, to obscure Divine power in its creation.

Now if there is any principle in the nature of creative work which will explain this obscure paradox, that the seemingly greatest creation of Divine power should be one which can defy that power, we evidently cannot find

it first in the case of the soul itself.   If we
could, we should not have had the problem.
We cannot really analyse the creation of the
soul, obscured as it is by the impenetrable
light of its creator, by the primeval mist of its
beginning, and by its present sin.   If we would
find some principle in the nature of a creation
which will explain this paradox, we must find
it first in some other realm, where its working
is self-evident.

And we do not have to look far for such a
realm, for the human soul itself has, as a
divinest portion of its birthright, the power to
create.   The "creative imagination" is the
perpetual mirror of the Creative Power which
made us.   This creative imagination, being of
the very fibre and substance of the soul, works
in every part of our lives, and in many cases
its workings cannot be disentangled from the
general strand of our activities.   The range of
its work runs from the most mechanical acts,
in which it plays a very minor part, up to those
acts which are pure creation.   For there are
acts in which the creative imagination is su-

preme, directing the whole man as its rapt and
inspired instrument, and in these acts it works
freely and truly according to the pure principles of creative work.

Nor do we have to look far for this truest
creative activity of man. It lies unquestionably in the arts, which are the peculiar province
of the creative imagination. This is so universally recognised that it is almost a sufficient
definition of the arts, in a broad sense, to say
that they are the creative work of man. In
them the creative imagination is in its king-
dom, not hampered by the chains of logic or
the purposes of the will, but directing intellect
and will as its servants, and bound only by its
own nature and its own higher law and logic.
It is, however, as we see at once, subject to
certain limitations of the senses through which
it must make its appeal to other minds. And
because of this necessity it must work in materials which are not its own creation, for by
these materials of sound or colour or form it
must touch the senses. To the extent to which
it must use these materials its purely creative

action is made, though not necessarily less
real, at least less visible. And the ways in
which these modes and mediums have affected
the purely creative character of the arts have
given rise to all the endless theories of art.
Just how shall the creative imagination appeal,
legitimately and effectively, to other minds,
and what are its proper relations to its materials of sound or colour or form? How far on
the one hand may the creative spirit transcend
its materials, and overleap the barriers between
one art and another? And how far on the
other hand shall it be restrained by the idiom
of the particular vehicle which it uses? These
questions, with which it is the work of theories
of art to deal, have very little to do with the
pure principles of creative work, which belong
to the nature of the soul itself and not to the
nature of its materials. And while creative
vigour varies not with the art but with the man
who wields the art, we may say that the art
which is least affected by modes and mediums,
which has the least of its work made ready to
its hand in already existent sound or colour or

solid substance, and is most sufficient to itself, is the most purely creative art.

And the most purely creative art, of which these things are true, stands out unmistakably from all the others. Its name marks it in this way. For the ancient Greeks, whose criticism was as perfect as their creative work, and whose divisions of the arts have never been outworn, when they distinguished the arts, named the artists by what the artists did, as sculptors, painters, architects, musicians, and their work they called sculpture, painting, architecture, music. But they separated one art from the others, and called those who practised it simply " poietai," " makers " or " creators," and their work " poiesis," " poesy," or " creation." The reason was that to them the poet, the maker, worked in pure creation. His works were not wrought out of materials, of form, or colour, or even of sound, for though they had sound, it was but a garment, and not, as in music, the living body itself of the art. They were bodied forth directly by the imagination, to which words were but symbols, and these symbols themselves the work of the creative imagination, partly of the people at large, and partly of the poet who fused and remoulded the words. The Greeks therefore, by a distinction which has never been questioned, called the art which dealt in no materials, but only in the imagination, " poetry," or " creation," and its artist " poietes," or " creator." Poetry is, indeed, the most simple and purely creative work known to man. We may look to find the principles of creative work most clearly revealed in poetry.

When we speak of the creative art of poetry, we remember at once that there is a certain line of cleavage in poetry. Some poetry is almost entirely a creation, and some is largely the expression of the soul. We have agreed, following the Greeks again, to call these two great classes of poetry dramatic and lyric, by a distinction lying in the very nature of poetry. Poetry may be defined sufficiently for our purposes as a creative expression of the soul; but lyric poetry is especially expression, the outpouring of the soul, while dramatic poetry, whose work is the imaging of other souls, whether in drama, epic, or other form, is essentially creation. All best poetry is both expression and creation; it is the truest expression of the soul, in the best creative and poetic form. Great lyric poetry, however outpouring or passionate, is never formless, but is clothed in noble or splendid form by the creative imagination, and great dramatic poetry is made alive and is fired by the life and passion of the poet's own soul. In all the highest works of poetry creation and expression are found in one.

It is because the life of poetry is the poet's own life that poetry cannot be made by rule. Poetry made in that way, as it was in the time of Pope, is instinct not with life but with rule and propriety. Neither for this reason can it be made, as many in recent times in France and England have tried to make it, by art alone. Such poetry, though the charm of art may preserve it as a perfect, melodious, highly coloured handiwork, will not live, and cannot be said even now to live, for it has not

the poet's own life in it. He moulded it,
and coloured it, and made it musical, but for-
got to put his soul into it. For the power of
poetry flows always from the poet's own life
of power, so that, as Milton says, to write
great poetry a man ought himself to be a true
poem. If we would find to what rapid fervour
or what aerial heights the poet's own soul may
bring his poetry, we need only to turn to Pin-
dar, with his rush of molten imagery, or to
Shelley, upborne on the winds of imagination,
skylark and eagle at once in one musical flight.
And if we would find the outbursts of the
poet's own heart reaching an unsurpassed pitch
of greatness, we may come to more than one
fierce apostrophe or adoring vision of Dante,
or to the storm of prophecy in Lycidas, or the
rapture and pathos of the blind Milton's hymn
to the uncreated light. If we may judge by the
past, poetry cannot go above such heights as
these, reached by the nature of the poet himself.

Yet we cannot stop here, and say that the
power of the poet's own life in his poetry is

the whole secret of greatness in poetry. Dante
with his " Rose of the Redeemed," and Milton
with his " Hail, Holy Light," may reach
diviner heights than Lear in the storm or Hector at the gate of the ships. Yet Homer and
Shakespeare, who are known to us almost entirely through creative forms, have rank un-
passed in that immortal company. For it is
as creators that they all have place in their
high collateral glory. Homer has held the
ages under his spell because he created a world,
of men and gods, of seas and lands. Shakespeare created, for his marvellous stage, not a
world, but human nature itself, individual and
universal. That which set the impress of the
" Divine Comedy" upon Europe, so that the
Renaissance was but the expanded soul of
Dante, was the vast and intense reality of his
work; it was the fact that those circles of hell,
that mount of purgation, those orbs of heaven,
and all that multitude of beings, lived, a new-
created world. And " Paradise Lost " has
moulded succeeding religion and character because Milton bodied forth by his creative imag-

ination a whole universe, so that men live in it to-day whether they will or not. The greatest power of the soul in poetry is shown, then, in creative forms. The world of Homer, the worlds of Dante, the human cosmos of Shakespeare, the religious universe of Milton, filled as they are with the life of the poet himself, are among the supreme works of creative power in poetry because they are, above all, creations.

In such creative works, filled by the creator's own life, and yet living as creations outside of and beyond himself, we have the highest attainments of human creative power. And as supreme works of the creative imagination they bear the creative stamp in every part. Even those outbursts in Dante and Milton, where the poet's own soul ascends almost beyond words, are clothed in creative forms. The poet's passion is revealed not in description of itself but in vivid depiction of the objects of the passion. And yet the passion is the poet's own. It is the poet's own soul which arises in such apocalypse before us. The soul is here revealing the great-

ness of its spiritual nature rather than the
greatness of its creative power. For the soul
reveals its creative power at its greatest when
at or near these heights of its own nature it
produces other souls, its creations, filled with
this same ardent life, and feeling these passions
and aspirations as their own. The creative
imagination can never, perhaps, lift any im-
agined soul into the greatest heights. Certainly neither Othello nor Lear nor any other
creation of man ever rose to the full soul-
height of Dante or Milton themselves. And if
the creative imagination could lift these im-
agined souls to the level of the highest actual
souls, it would exhaust the ideal of human
creation and attain the unattainable. But not
far below this highest point the creative poet,
the "maker," can do his greatest work. He
can make the souls which he images see with
their own eyes, think their own thoughts, speak
their own words, and feel the most poign-
ant, the most profound, the most inspired
passions as their very own. He can thus trans-
form his own most intense life into the life of

his creations. Then at last man has done his greatest creative work. For this power to bring into being, even though only in imagination, souls which are not our own, and which did not exist, and to make them live with a vitality which was ours, but has become theirs,—this power is, more than any other which is given to us, like the Power which made the universe, and created worlds out of we know not what, and brought into life, from its own life, beings who had not been.

The distinctive nature of this highest work of 'the creative poet, who creates souls which are not himself and which yet have life from his own life, is made still clearer by comparison with those creations which fall below the highest. The creative imagination is commonest in childhood, and in the child who lives in a world of picturesque and vivid unrealities we have a good example of a mind most imaginative, but only slightly creative. For while the child imagines many beings of many sorts, with a realism astonishing to us, it fills them all with its own naive and fanciful life, and gives to them its own feelings, its own views of things, and its own atmosphere. They do not live a distinct created existence; radiant, grotesque, gigantic, prosaic, they share alike the nature of the child. We do not need to go for similar instances in poetry to the many poets whose impulse is lyric, and who by preference sing rather than create, for among those whose work is in the creative forms we have an instance of a peculiar falling short of great creative work. This instance is Byron. We feel in his works a splendid and elemental force, a power and an intensity truly unknown to our day. And yet we feel in them an equal failure of creative power, for with all his power in them they are not distinct created personalities. His characters are for the most part but so many passionate aspects of Byron. Their personality, their thoughts, their feelings, are his. In this Byron is like the child whose imaginations all share the child's nature. But if it happens that the child, who, because he is a child, has something of the poet's nature, is to grow into a true poet, and a creative

poet, his creations become, with the growth of
his creative power, more and more distinct
from himself in personality. The greater his
creative power, the more his creations stand
out, objectively, as we say, having wholly their
own mind and character. And at last when
we come to those creations which the world has
chosen to call supreme, we find each one a
rounded, vivid, separate being, distinct alike
from the others and from the poet who created
them. Achilles, Hector, Ulysses, Lear, Hamlet, Othello, Iago, Mephistopheles, Milton's
Satan,—these supreme works of creative
power are in their personality almost entirely
distinct from their creators. We may say then
that, as we have found them, the greatest creative works are those which are most distinct
from their creators in personality. It is true
that these greatest creations are apart not only
from less distinct creations, but also from certain almost equally distinct characters of Euripides, Molière and Schiller, because these three
poets lacked in their own souls the sustained
vision of Homer, the intense religion of Dante,

the grandeur of Milton, the universal grasp
of Shakespeare.   And it is true also that three
of the supreme poets, Aeschylus, Sophocles,
Goethe, fall below the highest in their creations, because the souls of the great four are
above even these in loftiness, immensity and
ardour.   We must combine our principle of
distinct personality, then, as a measure of
greatness in a creation, with the condition that
this greatness also depends upon the greatness
of the life of the poet within the creation.   And
we may now formulate the principle of greatness in a creation as we have found it, in this,
that the greatest creation is that which, having
the greatest life from its creator, is most distinct from him in personality.

But by this principle the greatness of a creation varies not only with the poet's creative
power, but with the greatness of his spiritual
nature as seen in the creation.   If we could, in
order to have a test of creative power, regard
the greatness of the creator's spiritual nature
as a fixed quantity, we should have a principle
by which creations would be the measure sim-

ply of the creative power which wrought in
them. And this principle would be that, granting the creator's life in the creation, the greatest creation, as a work of creative power, is
that which is most distinct in personality from
the creator. And it appears that we may still
have an example of this simplified principle in
the work of the four supreme poets, and may
regard the life which they put into their creations as a fixed quantity. For, either because
they are all so far above us that we cannot
measure them, or because they are alike in
greatness of soul, we cannot declare that the
soul of any one of them, as revealed in his
creations, is greater than that of the others.
They are different, and we may have personal
preferences, but, so far as the world can tell,
they are equal. Finding then these creations
equal in the greatness of the poet's life in them,
we may look for the final distinction which the
creative principle of distinctness of personality
makes among them. And we find that the
creations of Shakespeare stand out as greater
than the others in this regard. Homer's figures

have lived through the ages, clear, individual, personal. Yet compared with the highest standard they all have a little of the characteristics of Homer. They all delight in the same things which Homer, as revealed in his own words, not theirs, delighted in. Dante's characters are of intense and vivid reality, each a distinct person; yet from the number of them, the short space in the poem given to each, and the fact that they all, however distinct, are heard through Dante's ears, and have the atmosphere of Dante's theme, the whole gallery of his characters has the effect of Dante's personality. If Dante's characters are all imperceptibly Dantesque, Milton's portraiture is all to a certain degree Miltonic. This may be partly because he deals less with personal beings than with spaces, worlds, chaos, Eden, Heaven and Hell; and still more because his personal beings are Divine or angelic, and therefore incapable of such distinctness of human personality in our thought, or else typical, like Adam and Eve, with any marked individuality as yet undeveloped. And even in

Satan, a distinct and gigantic personality, beyond anything in Dante because of the greater scale and length of the portrayal, something of his grandeur is somehow Milton's own, perverted into defiance of Milton's God. But Shakespeare's creations are to our eyes absolutely distinct in mind, and will, and habit, so much so that we hardly know from his plays what Shakespeare's personality was. Certainly if any one of his creations, Hamlet, for instance, is Shakespeare's own personality, then Othello, and Lear, and Macbeth, and a score of others, utterly distinct and dissimilar, cannot be. He has by his creative power transformed his own life in his works into what seem to us absolutely distinct personalities. And therefore, though he shows no greater soul of his own, and never rose perhaps to the heights which Dante or Milton attain, his creations are the greatest of all, because of their distinctness from himself. And the world, recognising that poetry is a creative art, has held Shakespeare as the greatest of all poets.

We have come, then, in the most creative

realm of human creative power, to this supreme principle, that the greatest creation is that which, having the fullest life from the creator, is most distinct from him in personality; the life the expression of his life, the distinctness the revelation of his creative power. It remains now for us to see whether this principle will explain the paradox of the defiant soul as God's apparently greatest creation.

VIII

THE WITNESS OF SIN

BEFORE we apply this principle, found in human creative work, to Divine creative work, we ought to make sure just what force the principle has there. It unquestionably has the force of analogy. For there is a very complete analogy between man's creative work and God's. Man's creative work is but the type and shadow of God's, with the one great difference between them that the creative imagination creates imaginary life and God creates real life. But its force is much greater than that of analogy. It does not depend upon a general likeness between human and Divine creative work, but lies rather in the very nature of creative work. The principle would doubtless be conclusive enough if it clearly revealed itself as true in the case of Divine creation which we wish explained. But we may also

find it self-evidently true, as an abstract principle, lying in the very nature of things, and of
creative work, and therefore absolutely conclusive if it explains the case of the defiant
soul as a Divine creation.

Let us take the principle: The greatest creation is that which, having the fullest life from
the creator, is most distinct from him in personality. Now it is clear, in regard to the
first part of the principle, that, in the nature of
things, the more of his own life a creator puts
into his creation, which has all its life from
him, the greater that living thing which he creates will be. And the greatest creation in this
respect will be that into which he has put the
most of his own life. The second part of the
principle, also, that of distinctness from the creator in personality, is equally self-evident.
For the more his creative power does in a creation, making it less and less a mere part of
himself, and more and more a distinct and separate created work, the greater work of creative power that creation will be. And of
course the greatest creation, as a work of cre-

ative power, will be that in which his creative power has wrought the most, and made the creation most distinctly a creation, and most distinct from himself. And as a whole, a creator's greatest creative work will be that in which, while he has put the most of his own life into it, and made it therefore a living being, his creative power has also wrought most, and made this living being most distinctly a creation and most distinct in personality from himself. The principle is self-evident, not only in human creative work, but as an abstract principle, in the very nature of things.

We may bring this principle as self-evident, then, to the case of that apparently Divine creation, the human soul. How does the principle affect the paradox, which is our problem of theodicy, that the soul of man, which defies God, seems yet His greatest known creation? Applied to this supreme case, the principle is more clearly and luminously evident than anywhere else. For in the first place man, as a creation of God, is more filled with his Maker's own life than is any other creation

which we know.   He differs in this from the
earth, the stars, the whole firmament, because
he has sentient life.   He is apart from all
unconscious life, as of plants, for he realizes.
He differs also by an immeasurable gulf from
all merely conscious animal life, for he has
personal life.   And beside all this he is conscious that he has immortal life, such as could
have come to him only from Divine life,
breathed into him by his Creator.   And yet,
for the other part of the principle, man, with
all this life from his Creator's life, is distinct
from his Creator in personality, so distinct
that he can even defy Him!   It seemed a
strange and profound paradox; but now it is
the most vivid embodiment which we know
of that creative principle of distinctness of
created personality.   Man is so distinct from
his Creator in personal mind, and personal will,
and personal power of choice, that he can actually work in opposition to his Maker's will, and
choose evil in defiance of Him and all His
power.   There could be no greater distinctness of personality, and no more striking exhi-

bition of the work of creative power than this
created free will which is thus able to defy
God.   Man becomes indeed the supreme evidence of Divine creative power.   We have but
to compare him with the vast inanimate universe, the visible evidence, we think, of God's
power, but which, though it has not God's
kind of life in it, can yet have no will but
God's will, while man, who has God's life in
him, yet has his own free will, able even to defy
God's will.   Leaving out higher orders of
moral beings, man is, of all things known to
us, the greatest work of the power of God,
which could create so free and distinct a personality.

That vague doubt, therefore, which is the
furthest and yet the most fundamental reach
of the question of defiant sin and God, the
doubt whether we can rationally see any
Divine power acting in the creation of the soul
which can defy a Divine Creator's power, is
dissolved by this new light.   The defiant sinning soul no longer obscures the Power which
it defies, for in its very defiance it appears as

a supreme work and revelation of that Power.
In the very distinctness of personality which
can act against its Creator's will, and defy
Him, the soul reveals His power.   The soul,
by its faculty of choice and its power of defiance, is a witness, and in its use of that power
of defiance an active witness, to the power of
God who made it.   It is, in this marvellous
freedom and distinctness of personality, almost a proof, if we logically needed a proof,
that God's power is omnipotence.   For it is
questionable whether anything but infinite
power could have so combined life from
God's own life with such completely distinct
and separate will.   But short of this, it is very
clear that the soul's defiance can raise no doubt
at all as to Divine power in its creation, but is
rather a witness, the highest witness in creation, to God's power.

We have therefore a theodicy of witness
to remove the obscuring doubt of God, as we
had a theodicy of defence to dissolve the
dilemma and its denial of God.   Sin, being
in spite of God, is now not only no denial that

God's goodness and power are infinite, but is a positive witness to His goodness and power. It invokes the testimony of conscience to the goodness of God. It arouses God's protest in natural evil, which is the protest of Divine goodness. And it exhibits His goodness in the creation of moral beings. For Divine goodness in all its breadth of holiness and love is revealed in the creation of moral beings with power to sin and consequent power to be holy. And though sin is in spite of God, it not only is no denial of Divine power, but is now a positive witness to His power. Restrained in regard to the soul by creative self-consistency, which denies neither perfect goodness nor omnipotence in Him, the Creator appears Divinely good and Divinely full of power in creating the free soul. As we see Divine goodness in the Creator's holy and loving purpose in creating moral beings with personal will, so equally we see Divine power in his ability to create such beings. In our souls, made to be holy, though now sinning, we see Divine good purpose carried out by Divine power. Our defiant power of choice, acting in spite of the Creator, praises Him in spite of itself. Our very sins, the perverted sinful outworkings of that faculty of choice, glorify Him with a cloud of unwilling voices. This is the witness of sin to God's goodness and God's power.

There remains but one question about the theodicy. In our souls, made to be holy, but now sinning in spite of God, we truly see Divine good purpose carried out by Divine power. This, with God's creative self-consistency, forms the whole theodicy of defence and of positive witness. But may there not be some final question of the reality of a Divine good purpose in the creation of souls for holiness, when we see no soul holy, but all unholy? And must not God's self-consistency as Creator, which keeps Him from breaking off His creative purpose, require also some carrying out of that purpose? And has not God laid some responsibility upon Himself in creating, even with a holy and loving purpose, a race of souls the possibility of whose sin He cannot prevent? These three questions are really one, and to them all there is but one answer, the Redemption.

For each of these questions, which concern not details but the general aspect and reality of the theodicy, finds its complete answer in the Redemption. In regard to the first question, of the reality of a Divine good purpose in the creation of human souls for holiness when we see no souls holy, but all unholy, we must admit the fairness of the question. We could not clearly see Divine good purpose in a purpose which ended entirely in ruin and failure, with no soul attaining holiness. It might not be in God's power to accomplish that purpose in every free soul; but with no soul attaining it, that holy purpose would seem unreal. But the redemption from sin into holiness gives reality to that creative purpose. For if God in creating moral beings with human holiness as the final aim foresees not only sin, but a final saving from sin, and a final holiness, through the Redemption, there can be no question of the reality of His good purpose in creating moral beings.

The next question concerns the complete reality of that creative self-consistency which dissolves the dilemma of sin. If God's self-consistency restrains Him, in the case of these sinning souls, because He cannot rationally destroy them with His creative purpose wholly unaccomplished, must not the same self-consistency require at least some final accomplishment of that great and holy purpose? It certainly seems so, and the answer again is found in the Redemption? For in the Redemption there is some final accomplishment, and the largest one possible, of that purpose. We cannot demand, either for His self-consistency, or for the reality of His creative purpose, that He should be able to accomplish that purpose in all the defiant souls of the race. Any real accomplishment of that purpose meets the demand of reason.

And the third question concerns the complete reality of Divine goodness, in face of sin, in this theodicy. For though sin is in spite of God, and His purpose in creating souls which can sin is wholly good, does He not lay

some responsibility for sin upon Himself, in
creating, even with a holy and loving purpose,
a race of souls the possibility of whose sin,
and the foreseen actuality of whose sin, He
cannot prevent? The answer to this question,
as we have already seen in first speaking of
God's creative purpose,[1] lies also in the Redemption. It is doubtful how great that
responsibility is. For His creative purpose
does not and cannot include sin. Man makes
sin. God but forsees it, and His only responsibility is the very remote one that He creates,
with a holy and loving purpose, a race of beings
the possibility of whose foreseen wilful sin He
cannot in His self-consistency directly prevent.
But He does by the Redemption make the only
direct prevention of sin possible to Him. And
His creative purpose, although it does not include sin, does include the Redemption. And
He meets His mere shadow of responsibility,
incurred also as it is with a loving purpose, by
the overwhelming gift of Himself. In the
light of this sacrifice of Himself in the person

[1] Chapter IV.

of His Son dearer than Himself upon the cross, God's purpose and plan of creation appears, both to the heart and to the reason, infinitely more wondrous in goodness and love than if it meant no sin and included no Redemption. Divine holiness and love are visible already in God's purpose in the soul, but when they are carried out into complete reality in the Redemption they become glorious beyond all thought.

The Redemption sets then the final seal of reality upon the theodicy. It gives complete reality to the holy purpose of the soul's creation, and reveals completely the self-consistency of the Creator, and dissolves the last doubt of His goodness in creating souls which can sin. In finding in the Redemption the final reality of the theodicy, we are not trying to make the theodicy contribute to the Redemption. It is for us to take whatever is needed, and can rationally be so taken, for the true theodicy; and the Redemption, the great doctrine of Christianity, is needed for the reality of the theodicy, and is in harmony with all the terms of the problem, the goodness of God, the power of God, the self-consistency of God, and the freedom and sin of the soul. If we reject that truth of the Redemption, simply because it is revealed religion, we lose all hope of a true and real theodicy. If we desire a theodicy absolutely real as well as complete, we must take the Redemption. It is true that the Redemption is by no means, as some seem to think, a theodicy in itself. The saving of souls from sin, even if all souls could be saved, is not an explanation of sin. The Redemption is meant to be in itself not an explanation of sin, but a way of escape from sin. But it is the crowning reality of the theodicy.

The Redemption or Atonement is the crowning reality of the theodicy because it is the carrying out of the great creative purpose. It cannot be called in itself the purpose of the creation, but is rather a part, and perhaps, in its exercise of Divine goodness at least, the largest part of the creative work. For the creative purpose, meaningless and incomplete without it, is with it complete and glorious. Creation and Redemption are in the largest

sense one great creative work, the creation of a universe of free and adoring beings,
of which the first creation is the beginning and
the Redemption is the climax. Certainly this
is rational, for the Redemption is as consistent
with the holiness and love and power of God
as the first creation is, and is a rational and
consistent carrying out of the creative purpose.
And it is of the greatest import that the Scriptures, which reveal the Redemption, show it as
the climax of the creative work, and the Creator and the Redeemer as one and the same
person, even among the united persons of the
Trinity. Christ, the Son, the Logos, who is
the Redeemer, is also the Creator. "For,"
says John, "all things were made through
Him, and without Him was not anything made
that hath been made." And Paul declares,
"For in Him were all things created, in the
heavens and upon the earth, things visible and
things invisible." Creator and Redeemer are
one, as creation and Redemption are one. He
makes holy in the Redemption those whom
He made free and moral in the creation. And

He makes them free again, the Scripture says, from the bondage of the will in sin. "If any man is in Christ," it is declared, he is therefore "a new creation." And in one profound sentence, seldom understood, the Scripture gathers up this whole true theodicy, showing how in the Redemption the Creator and Redeemer finishes and makes eternal His great creative work; "for by one offering He hath perfected forever them who are made holy." And again in the Apocalypse, in the great hymn of the theodicy before the throne of God, beginning with the worship of Deity, and proceeding in choruses of ever-increasing multitudes, through the Creation,—"for thou didst create all things, and because of thy will they were, and were created,"—and the Redemption,—"for thou wast slain, and didst purchase with thy blood men of every tribe,"—and the adoration of "the Lamb that hath been slain,"—to the chant of the whole animate universe "unto Him that sitteth upon the throne, and unto the Lamb," the Redeemer,—in this hymn, as profound and as broad in its history of the uni-

verse as the Epistle to the Romans, is revealed
the whole sweep of the Divine creative work.

It is rational to take the testimony of the
Scriptures, which reveal to us all that we really
know of either creation or Redemption, and
which make the two one great creative and
successive work.   But simply for the theodicy,
this supreme problem of human thought, this
problem of the goodness and power of God,
the Redemption is the final and logical reality.
It gives to the complete theodicy the breath of
life.   We see the Creator revealed in goodness
and power in the creation of the soul which can
sin, unable consistently to prevent sin by coercion, but protesting against it in natural evil,
and carrying out His creation, His consistency,
His protest, and His purpose, and supremely
revealing his goodness and power, in the
Redemption.

The Universal Elements of the Christian Religion

12mo, Cloth, net $1.25.   **CHARLES CUTHBERT HALL**

Amid the flood of books on the subject of religion there appears every few years one book that dwarfs all others, one that crystalizes the thinking of the Christian world. Such is this book. This man separates himself from the bewildering crossed paths and standing free, grasps clearly the course that is being followed by the Christian age of which he is a part. His knowledge is cosmopolitan and accurate, his logic is clean cut and simple, and his conclusions convincing and optimistic, springing from a faith at once simple and profound in its certainty that Jesus Christ is the Saviour of the world of men who are his possession.

Paths to Power

2nd Edition. 12mo, Cloth, net $1.25.   **F. W. GUNSAULUS**

"Not till now has Dr. Gunsaulus put a volume of his discourses into print. On reading them one is disposed to concede his right to the place assigned him by Prof. Wilkinson in the list with such men as Belcher, Brooks and Spurgeon. Dr. Gunsaulus resembles Dr. Joseph Parker in the vivifying imagination which he brings to the exposition of his texts, and is a master in allegorizing from them, fresh and profound lessons."—*The Outlook.*

Humanity and God   And other Sermons.
12mo, Cloth, net $1.50.   **SAMUEL CHADWICK**

"In every sermon the preacher looks at man in the light of God and strives to show that in the visitation of God in Christ the hope of humanity centres. The author treats with great force and freshness a subject on which plain practical teaching is in our own time much needed."—*Methodist Times.*

Loyalty: The Soul of Religion

12mo, Cloth, net $1.00.   **J. G. K. McCLURE**

"Dr. McClure sets forth the idea with a clearness not surpassed in terature, and in a great variety of illustration, argument and appeal. . . . a great book to give to a young man of the college type. It takes him as he is and takes hold of best possibilities in him."—*N. Y. Observer.*

Our Attitude as Pastors   Toward Modern Biblical Criticism

Paper, net 10c   **PROF. LOUIS RUFFET**

An address to the students of the Theological Seminary of the Free Evangelical Church, of Geneva, Switzerland.

EVANGELISTIC.

The Evangelistic Note A study of needs and methods, together with a series of direct appeals.

3rd Edition. 12mo, Cloth, net $1.25. **W. J. DAWSON**

"One of the most remarkable and stirring of recent books. It is really the story of a great crisis in the life of a great preacher. Mr. Dawson's experience in his own church has justified his faith, and his book is a most stimulating treatise on homiletics and pastoral theology. It is epoch-making in character."—*The Watchman.*

Torrey and Alexander The Story of a World-Wide Revival

A record and study of the work and personality of the Evangelists DR. R. A. TORREY, D. D., and CHARLES M. ALEXANDER.

Illustrated, 12mo, Cloth, net $1.00. **GEORGE T. B. DAVIS**

The multitudes who have followed the marvellous progress of the religious awakening in Australasia, India, and Great Britain, accompanying the efforts of these evangelists will eagerly welcome this glimpse from the inside of their career, personality and work. Mr. Davis has been associated in a confidential capacity with the work of the two evangelists, and writes with keen appreciation of the interesting facts in stirring language.

Real Salvation and Whole-Hearted Service A second volume of Revival Addresses.

12mo, Cloth, net $1.00. **R. A. TORREY**

The multitudes led to decision in connection with the preaching of these sermons, gives assurance that their influence will be extended far beyond the reach of the speaker's voice. Positive conviction and a loving plea as from a God-sent messenger, are the marked features of this new volume.

Talks to Men About the Bible and the Christ of the Bible.

12mo, Cloth, net 75c. **R. A. TORREY**

"The directness, simplicity, with wide scholarship and literary charm of these talks, and unhesitating claim for the highest and fullest inspiration, inerrancy and authority for the Bible, make them trumpet calls to faith."—*N. Y. Observer.*

The Passion for Souls

16mo, Cloth, net 50c. **J. H. JOWETT**

Seven sermons on tenderness, watchfulness, companionship, rest and vision of the apostle Paul's passion for human souls. This little volume shows his keen, reverent insight at its best and is made rich with abundant and well chosen illustrations.

The Worker's Weapon It's Perfection, Authority and Use.

16mo, Cloth, net 25 cents. **JOHN H. ELLIOTT**

"A fine presentation of the unquestionable authority of God's Word and pointed and clear directions and illustrations of how to study and use the Bible."

The Witness of Sin A Theodicy
12mo, Cloth, net $1.00.   NATHAN ROBINSON WOOD

A splendidly thought-out presentation of the problem presented by the presence of sin in a world dominated by God. Some sort of a theodicy, some conception of the solution of this question is necessary to any religious thinking. Mr. Wood's work is a marked addition to present-day theology.

The Walk, Conversation and Character of Jesus Christ Our Lord
12mo, Cloth, net $1.50.   ALEXANDER WHYTE

"Rich and glowing meditations on the life of our Lord. A genuine contribution to Christology. What distinguishes it most is the author's singularly clear perception of Christ alone without sin. While always in touch with real life, Dr. Whyte has that power of separating himself from the stream of things which is essential to a great religious teacher."—*British Weekly (Robertson Nicoll, Editor.)*

Jesus of Nazareth, the Anointed of God
Or, The Inner History of a Consecrated Life.
12mo, Cloth, net 75c.   P. COOK, M.A.

"As a brief and concise summary, a bird's-eye view of the life of Jesus this volume will be of value."—*Reformed Church Messenger.*

The Divine Tragedy A Drama of the Christ
12mo. Cloth, net, $1.00.   PEYTON H. HOGE

The author's ambition is "to tell in the most vivid and practical form for men living in the world to-day the story of Jesus of Nazareth in its culminating scenes." One could exhaust adjectives in praise of the author's management of the dramatic form and his blank verse. It is a wonderful work. The dedicatory poem alone is of such surpassing beauty that one will never forget it.

The Directory of the Devout Life
A Commentary on the Sermon on the Mount.
12mo, Cloth, net $1.00.   F. B. MEYER, M.A.

"In many respects the best writings Mr. Meyer has issued. They are eminently practical, and the pointed and piercing ideas of the Master are explained and brought home to personal character and life in an illuminating and stimulating way."—*Watchman.*

With the Sorrowing A Pastor's Handbook.
16mo, Cloth flex., net 75 cts.   Edited by F. W. PALMER

Presented with confidence to pastors, missionaries and other visitors in the homes of sorrow, as likely to prove a most valuable aid in their trying experiences. Although primarily a service book for funerals, it is vastly more than this. With Scripture selections of exceptional suggestive values and a collection of poems of comfort both rare and striking the little volume will be greatly prized.

DEVOTIONAL STUDIES.

The Christt of To-Day What? Whence? Whither?
16mo, Boards, net 50c. **G. CAMPBELL MORGAN**

A study originally presented from the platform of the Northfield Conferences, awakening exceptional interest at the time. No more suggestive work has appeared from Dr. Morgan's pen.

The Redeemed Life After Death
16mo, Boards, net 50c. **CHARLES CUTHBERT HALL**

Not a new theory of Immortality or a review of old theories, but a presentation with rare literary charm and with the comprehension of wide scholarship, of the grip of the Christian heart upon the life to come. It will comfort and assure the sorrowing, guide and convince the inquiring.

Moments of Silence
12mo, Cloth, net $1.25. **ALEXANDER SMELLIE, M.A.**

A book of daily meditations for a year.

Yet Another Day
32mo, Cloth, net, 25c. Leather, net, 35c. **J. H. JOWETT, M.A.**

A brief prayer for every day of the year, and it is not too much to say that, although scarcely any one of them contains one hundred words and most of them far less, they will drive straight to the heart as nothing that ever came from Mr. Jowett's pen. It is an extraordinary, little book, the flower of the sweetest, open eyed love of Christ. The impression of a single page is indelible.

The Inner Chamber of the Inner Life
12mo, Cloth, net 75c. **ANDREW MURRAY**

Suggests thoughts of the utmost importance as to the daily need of retirement, the true spirit of prayer, the fellowship with God, and kindred topics.

Inter-Communion With God
12mo, Cloth, net $1.00. **MARSHALL P. TALLING, PH.D.**

"Follows the theme of 'Extempore prayer,' along wider and higher lines. In the present book, true prayer is shown to be an approach from both the human and the divine sides."—*The Westminster*.

Bible Etchings of Immortality
12mo, Cloth, decorated, net 50c. **CAMDEN M. COBERN**

"The consolatory character of this little book makes it a suitable gift to a bereaved friend."—*Outlook*.

Scripture Selections to Memorize
With hanger, net $1.00. **HELEN MILLER GOULD**

A Wall Roll of passages emphasizing the power and love of God, the dignity of man, Christ as teacher, Redeemer, King. The life of the Christian, his duties, his final reward; prayer; worship; love. Selections from the Old and New Testaments, most helpful in strengthening faith, and deepening personal devotion.

How to Conduct a Sunday School

2nd Edition. 12mo, Cloth, net $1.25.   MARION LAWRANCE

General Secretary of the International Sunday School Association

"Packed full of useful information. Filled with details, specific and practical, for which a host of workers have longed and prayed. The book gives the cream of life-long experience and observation. In its concrete details lies its unique and practical service."—*The Examiner.*

Pencil Points for Preacher and Teacher

With an Introduction by Rev. Robert S. McArthur, D.D.

Illustrated, Cloth, net $1.25.   ROBERT F. Y. PIERCE

Dr. Pierce is the recognized exponent of the art of conveying Scripture truth by means of blackboard sketches and object lessons. Crowded with illustrations of blackboard drawings and suggestions and forms a fitting companion to his popular book, "Pictured Truth."

Kindergarten Bible Stories Old Testament.

Illustrated, 12mo, Cloth, net $1.25.   By LAURA E. CRAGIN.

Devoted to the stories of which the little folks never tire, but told in the inimitable style for which this author has an exceptional gift as well as a peculiar discernment in bringing out the lesson of value.

How to Plan a Lesson And other Talks to Sunday School Teachers.

2nd Edition. 16mo, Cloth, net 50c.   MARIANNA C. BROWN

"Suggestive, interesting, valuable......The writer is an experienced teacher, who has made proof of her theories, and who is well able to make valuable suggestions."—*Herald and Presbyter.*

The Gist of the Lesson—1906

Leather, net 25c (*Vest pocket size*)   R. A. TORREY
Interleaved, Leather, net 50c

The seventh annual issue of this multum in parvo upon the International Sunday School lessons. A most popular exposition. Nearly fifty thousand copies sold annually.

Practical S. S. Lesson Commentary For 1906

Carefully prepared by specialists in the various departments with Map and Blackboard exercises. 8vo, Cloth, 50c. net, postage extra.

Its practical value and marked spiritual expositions have given it a permanent place.   FOURTEENTH YEAR.

The Twentieth Century New Testament

Final Revised Translation 1905.

Cloth, net $1.00; Morocco, net $1.50; Morocco, gilt edges, net $2.00. Morocco Divinity Circuit, net $3.50; India Paper Edition, net $5.00.

All criticism has now been carefully considered and the results embodied in the New Revised and Final Edition. This is the product of thirteen years labor by a score of translators and is practically a new translation.

HISTORICAL, REFERENCE, TEXT BOOKS.

The History of the Reformation of Religion in Scotland With which are included Knox's confession and the book of Discipline. A Twentieth Century Edition. Revised and edited by Cuthbert Lennox, with frontispiece portrait.

Illustrated, 8vo, Cloth, net $2.00.   JOHN KNOX

This is a classic prepared for modern readers. Thomas Carlyle said of Knox's history: "The story of this great epoch is nowhere to be found as impressively narrated as in this book of Knox's."

History Unveiling Prophecy; or, Time as an Interpreter.

8vo, Cloth, net $2.00.   H. GRATTAN GUINNESS

A far-seeing study of the gradual unveiling of the meaning of the Apocalypse of St. John as it may be discovered in the events of the intervening centuries.

The Treasury of Scripture Knowledge

New Edition. 8vo, Cloth, $2.00

Introduction by R. A. TORREY

"In preparing notes on the Bible Lessons and on the books of the Bible, I have found more help in the *Treasury of Scripture Knowledge* than in all other books put together. I have recommended the use of this book to many people, and in after years they have thanked me for calling their attention to it. Their experiences with it have been similar to mine."—*R. A. Torrey.*

The Cyclopedic Handbook to the Bible

An introduction to the study of the Scriptures by the late Joseph Angus, M.A., M.D., thoroughly revised and in part rewritten by

8vo, Cloth, net $2.00.   SAMUEL G. GREEN

"In its present revised form much has been added from the gain acquired by a half-century of increasing knowledge, while the original plan, with some rearrangement, remains the same."—*The Outlook.*

Old Testament Introduction General and Special.

8vo, Cloth, net $2.00.   JOHN HOWARD RAVEN

A scholarly work that is marked by unusual clearness and attractive style. The author holds that the traditional view of the Old Testament has nothing to fear except from the ignorance and prejudice of its adherents. He has prepared a conservative text book that covers the whole field, with the view of avoiding both over-conciseness and diffuseness.

Exposition of the Apostle's Creed

Guild Text Books. *15th Thousand.*
16mo, cloth, net 40c; paper, net 25c   J. DODDS

Supplies a real need. It contains a careful, well-informed and well-balanced statement of the doctrines of the Church which are expressed or indicated in the Creed, will be helpful to many as arranging the passages of Scripture on which these doctrines rest.

NOV 24 1905

CPSIA information can be obtained
at www.ICGtesting.com
Printed in the USA
LVHW080204271119
638684LV00007B/152/P

9 781371 039899